SNAPREVISE

SnapRevise Text Guide:
In Cold Blood
by Truman Capote

Lauren White

InStudent Education UK Ltd owner of SnapRevise® trademark.
43 Priston Close, Worle, BS22 7FL, Weston-Super-Mare, United Kingdom

www.snaprevise.co.uk

Title: In Cold Blood by Truman Capote Text Guide
ISBN: 978-1-917424-25-7

Published by InStudent Education UK Ltd CN 15550989 under licence from InStudent Publishing Pty Ltd.
ACN 624 188101

Preface

In Cold Blood is a fantastic book, but it's also an incredibly complex one to analyse. Based on the real-life murders of the Clutter family in Kansas, 1959, Capote's melding of fact, fiction, literary journalism, and documentary-style storytelling makes for a layered narrative with a cacophony of voices. It also explicitly engages with highly contentious issues like the ethics of the death penalty and whether a punishment can ever fit a crime, as well as questions surrounding the agency of mentally ill criminals and whether they can be held responsible for their own actions.

This is a text steeped in history, horror, and honesty, and is the progenitor of modern true crime as we know it. It is also a very cerebral novel, tying together a range of stories to craft a nuanced narrative with so much to explore.

This Text Guide is designed to guide you through that complexity and give you a range of ideas and examples to discuss in your own writing. I hope you enjoy analysing *In Cold Blood* as much as I have!

— Lauren White

Contents

Section 1

Nutshell Summary

In Cold Blood is the story of an apparently motiveless murder of an innocent family, and the ramifications for the town and people involved. The full title of the text is *In Cold Blood: A True Account of a Multiple Murder and its Consequences,* which hints at Capote's dual focus on both the crime and its **reverberations**. But it is also a text that combines the credibility of a real story, the freedom of a documentary, the allure of a film, and the precision of poetry. This **synthesis** of genres and styles is something we will examine throughout this Text Guide, and is always worth keeping in mind when we talk about the narrative itself.

Reverberations: resonance or resounding consequences, like a ripple effect.

Synthesis: a combination of components forming a collective whole.

The Clutter family – Mr Herb Clutter and Mrs Bonnie Clutter, and their two youngest children Nancy and Kenyon – were brutally killed in their Kansas farm home on Sunday 15 November, 1959. The murderers were Perry Smith and Dick Hickock, two ex-convicts out on parole for petty theft who had heard rumours in prison that Mr Clutter kept $10,000 in a safe in his home, though this turns out to be false information. The two men plan to carry out a robbery, but leave having shot four innocent people.

From here, the book makes **temporal** shifts between the town of Holcomb where the Clutters lived and where the townsfolk struggle to accept and understand the violent and seemingly random attack in their community, and the stories of Dick and Perry who flee the state but are later apprehended by the Kansas Bureau of Investigation, led by investigator Alvin Dewey who was a friend of the Clutter family.

Temporal: relating to time.

Over the course of Dick and Perry's interactions, we learn more about their lives and the various tragedies and accidents that have befallen them, leaving them fractured and damaged both physically and psychologically. In the end, they are sentenced to death and held on Death Row in a Kansas prison for years before they are executed on April 14th, 1965.

The text opens with the introduction to and immediate murder of the Clutters, and ends with the execution by hanging of Perry and Dick. Hence, the story is **bookended** by death, but also concerns itself with what caused these events and what happens as a consequence. In this sense, this is almost like a mystery novel: we know that Perry and Dick were killed because they murdered the Clutters, but why were the Clutters murdered? This is the central premise that Capote seeks to unravel.

Bookended: supported on either side by something (like books on a bookshelf).

Section 2

Background Information

This text requires quite a bit of background knowledge to wade through before we get to the text itself. I would recommend starting with this section before analysing the text, and potentially even before you read the book itself as this may preempt many questions about how or why things occur, and will give you some idea of things to look out for as you read.

About the author

Truman Capote (1924–1984) was an American author who wrote *In Cold Blood* in 1966, seven years after the Clutter murders. His previous novella *Breakfast at Tiffany's* had earned him some acclaim, but *In Cold Blood* would skyrocket him to international bestseller status. He was also close friends with the author of *To Kill A Mockingbird* Harper Lee, who worked with Capote while he was researching the Clutter case.

After seeing a news article about the then unexplained murders in 1959, Capote and Lee visited Holcomb to meet with the individuals affected and investigate the events that took place. Capote would later look back on this experience as being incredibly lonely and difficult, not least because he was a flamboyant and openly gay man in a time and place where these things were wildly unacceptable. Later, when Perry and Dick were arrested by Kansas police, Capote would interview them in order to better understand their perspective. He got along well with Perry in particular, and maintained correspondence with him for five years before he was executed. This long wait would cause Capote some grief, as some say he wanted the book to end with the deaths of Perry and Dick to provide a sense of finality and closure, but over the course of his investigations, he realised he did not personally think Perry deserved to die.

In Cold Blood would be the last novel Capote ever wrote, and he spent the remaining 18 years of his life addicted to drugs and alcohol before dying at the age of 59.

About the book

Capote is a meticulous writer – we will see this later when exploring his prose, but this is also evident in the stories surrounding his composition of the text. In conducting his four year research into the murders and their consequences, Capote would take over 8,000 pages of notes, interviewing countless people in Holocomb and members of law enforcement. Even after *In Cold Blood's* publication, Capote had an eye for detail, suggesting that his publisher's front cover design featuring a drop of red blood should be changed to a darker shade of red, as though the blood had congealed, as a symbol for how time had passed since the murders had taken place. This kind of fastidiousness no doubt contributed to the text's commercial success, and has enshrined it as a seminal work of true crime non-fiction.

Key Point :
I would highly recommend watching Richard Brooks' 1967 film adaptation of *In Cold Blood,* as it is a very faithful rendition of Capote's work (though there are some departures, and you still need to read the book!).

Accuracy and veracity

When *In Cold Blood* was first published, it was heralded for its starkly accurate storytelling with many critics citing Capote's 8,000 pages of research notes as irrevocable proof that he had discovered and recounted everything accurately. However, he would also remark that he did not need to take notes during interviews because of his very impressive memory, which inevitably led some critics to question the **veracity** of his recollections. Whilst the text is undeniably one of the most precise true crime narratives, there were some inconsistencies between Capote's text and other historical records or anecdotal information.

Veracity: whether something conforms to facts and is accurate.

Below is a list of some of the differences between *In Cold Blood* and the real life story of the Clutters and their killers:

- The most controversial difference is Capote's favourable depiction of Dewey, the lead investigator, who is arguably the hero of the text, when in reality, official records show Dewey likely made a few mistakes in his pursuit of the case that the book did not delve into, such as his dogged misconception that the crime was committed by someone with a grudge against the Clutter family.
- The book also does not mention that Dewey and the Kansas Bureau of Investigation waited for five days before following up in the information that would lead to the capture of Perry and Dick during which time it is thought they may have committed four additional murders (another couple and their two young children) in Florida.
- Bonnie Clutter's psychological state is said to have been not as dire as is portrayed in the text. Her character in the novel is effectively an invalid, unable to leave her bed for days on end, though this was apparently a slight exaggeration.
- Capote includes some minor scenes that never occurred, such as Alvin Dewey visiting Nancy's grave and talking to Susan Kidwell at the end of the novel.

Beyond this, the text is incredibly true-to-life; however, the fact that Capote was so insistent on the fact that "every word" in his book was true opened him up to criticism. Fittingly, for a story about mankind's desperate search for meaning, the veracity of the book is something readers may never be fully sure about, as there are conflicting reports by Capote, the individuals he interviewed, and people who subsequently interviewed these people after the book's publication.

But many of the claims about Capote fabricating stories or constructing misleading narratives were based on hearsay and a somewhat contrarian approach intended to completely dismantle the book through cherry-picking specific evidence (i.e. proving that he got a quote wrong doesn't really destroy the fabric of the story; it just casts doubts). That is not to say all of these concerns were unfounded, but this does speak to the **subjectivity of storytelling** – Capote's text is a testament to his extensive research and understanding of the causes and consequences of the crimes, but there are inevitably elements of every character's story he cannot account for.

Eventually, Capote would admit to "fictionalising reality" to some extent, but maintained his novel was factually accurate and a faithful rendition of the story he so diligently researched.

Corrective power of true crime

We are currently in a kind of renaissance of the true crime genre – from books to films to podcasts to Neflix specials, there is something undeniably fascinating about these 'cases.' However, the way they are presented is vitally important to how we perceive the facts, and much of today's true crime media can trace their heritage back to the publication of *In Cold Blood.*

Most famously, the 2014 podcast *Serial* examined a 1999 murder of a young American student, Hae Min Lee, for which her classmate Adnan Syed was convicted. Although the podcast hosts never explicitly said Adnan was definitely innocent, their examination of the inconsistencies in the investigation and the way they portrayed Adnan and the other parties involved led to substantial public outcry over the perceived conviction of an innocent boy. The show's hosts would also visit Adnan in prison just as Capote had done with Perry, and both Capote and the *Serial* hosts would be criticised for forming too close an attachment with alleged killers, leading to a more sympathetic portrayal in the narratives they created. The podcast won several awards, and arguably revitalised the true crime genre in mainstream media.

The Netflix documentary *Making a Murderer* followed in this same mould, examining a 'cold' case for which someone had been wrongfully or dubiously convicted. This sparked a great deal of debate over the nature of the criminal justice system, just as Capote's novel did back in its day. Another show, *The Jinx* (my personal favourite!) was actually responsible for capturing the hitherto uncaught murderer's confession on film, leading to his arrest the day before the final episode aired.

However, as engrossing as these stories are to read or absorb, we should consider how these works encourage audience speculation and discussion about who is guilty and who is innocent, even though we cannot possibly be in possession of all the facts. This amateur sleuthing can have disastrous consequences, as the storytellers can largely shape public perception however they wish.

About the setting

The majority of the novel is set in the 1950s American South, particularly Kansas, though it jumps around to multiple places in Perry and Dick's memories as they flee the state after the murders. The town of Holcomb is the primary backdrop for the events in the text, and Capote spends a great deal of time describing its physical and emotional landscape. Ultimately though, Holcomb is a **microcosm** for rural America in its normalcy, and the way Capote captures the town's confusion and disbelief at this senseless, violent crime mirrors the response of all readers. For if this can happen in Holcomb, Capote implies, it can happen anywhere.

Microcosm: a small representation of a bigger picture concept.

The socio-cultural setting of the novel is also important, as it is grounded in the hallmarks of 1950s America and the American Dream. The character of Mr Clutter is the **epitome** of the admirable **patriarch** who works hard, loves his family, and pays his employees well, while his daughter Nancy is the stereotypical golden girl who gets straight-As, teaches their neighbours' daughters how to bake pies, and is involved in every extracurricular activity available to her. This further augments Capote's message about the indiscriminate nature of tragedy; in other words, if it can happen to the Clutters, it can happen to anyone.

Epitome: the perfect example of something.

Patriarch: the male leader or head of a household.

M'Naghten Rule

The M'Naghten Rule is a legal precedent used when juries deliberate on cases where a criminal is thought to be mentally insane. The rule states:

> QUOTES :
> "That **every man is to be presumed to be sane,** and... that to establish a defence on the ground of insanity, it must be clearly proved that, at the time of the committing of the act, the party accused was labouring under **such a defect of reason,** from disease of the mind, **as not to know the nature and quality of the act he was doing;** or if he did know it, that **he did not know he was doing what was wrong"**

In other words, a defendant could not be considered "insane" if they could discriminate between right and wrong. Essentially, this rule allows the justice system to judge someone "guilty but insane" if they did have the intent to commit the crime, as opposed to other systems like in the UK and many other countries which stipulate that if someone is insane, they are "not guilty by reason of insanity." Kansas is one of the few states in America that still use the M'Naghten Rule today, though this does not apply if a defendant is unable to form the intent to commit a crime. In the novel, Perry shows many signs of mental instability, and Capote criticises the M'Naghten Rule as being "a formula quite colour-blind to any gradations between black and white.'

Section 3

Chapter-by-Chapter Analysis

Epigraph

The text's epigraph is an excerpt taken from Francois Villon's *Ballade des pendus* (Ballad of the hanged). Translated into English, it reads:

Quotes :
"Human brothers who live after us,
Do not have your hearts hardened against us,
For, if you take pity on us poor ones,
God will sooner have mercy on you."

Villon was a French poet from the 15th century who engaged in a number of criminal activities. Towards the end of his life, he was arrested for petty theft and sentenced to death by hanging, though this was later reduced to a penalty of banishment. This poem was supposedly written while Villon was on death row, and hence deals with the ethics of capital punishment from the perspective of one of its would-be victims. In these opening lines, Villon is pleading with all "human brothers" (though most importantly the institutional authorities) to "take pity on us poor ones" so that they will likewise be shown God's mercy. Unsurprisingly, this poem is not in favour of the death penalty, but if we consider its message more broadly, it is also an appeal to readers to not "harden" our hearts against others, particularly those who are now dead or who were in some way "poor" in life. By evoking questions about human empathy and fairness, Capote sets the tone for the text and also foreshadows the **complicated matters of mercy and justice** yet to come.

The Last to See Them Alive

Key Point :
The chapters in *In Cold Blood* are quite long, so I have broken these up into sub-sections to help you navigate this analysis in relation to the events in the text!

This chapter title is a particularly morbid kind of foreshadowing – we have not even been introduced to "them," and already we know their deaths are inevitable. This lends the entire chapter an eerie, morose atmosphere, as we are told this information is merely the backdrop to the crimes that will be committed.

Introducing Holcomb and Herb

Capote opens by establishing the setting and landscape of Holcomb, a town so "lonesome" that it is colloquially known as "out there." It is a place of "hard blue skies," connoting intensity and purity, with "grain elevators rising as gracefully as Greek temples."

This **idyllic** description befits Capote's aggrandising of Holcomb as an epitome of American "Far West" identity; the fact that the town can be "seen from great distances" but in ways that make it look like merely an "aimless congregation of buildings" further implies that there is an intrinsic heart of Holcomb that outsiders struggle to grasp, but this is precisely what Capote intends to capture.

This is also where we get the first hints of **dilapidation** and the sense of loss and decay that afflicts the town. There is an electric 'dance' sign, "but the dancing has ceased." There is another "irrelevant" sign for the Holcomb bank which "failed in 1933," and this is followed with the almost facetious "and that, really, is all." This is a glimpse of a typical rural town, but before we can adjust to this familiar setting, Capote ominously reminds us that "until one morning in mid-November of 1959, few Americans... had ever heard of Holcomb." It was on this fateful day that the natural landscape of "coyotes," "tumbleweed," and "locomotive whistles" was interrupted by the "foreign sounds" of "four shotgun blasts that, all told, ended six human lives." With the advantage of hindsight, we know this is because Dick and Perry shot four of the Clutters and then were later executed for these crimes, but at this point, the intrigue of how four shots killed six people only adds to the suspense. This is also where Capote subtly hints at the aftermath of the events as people re-imagine the "sombre explosions that stimulated fires of mistrust" amongst neighbours that come to regard one another with suspicion and "as strangers."

Idyllic: extremely happy, peaceful, idealised, or perfectly blissful.

Dilapidation: falling into decay or disrepair.

We are then introduced to Herb Clutter as the master of River Valley Farm: he is 48, average height, and a "man's man." Capote goes into great detail about his physical appearance, characterising him as having a "healthy-hued youthfulness" and a strong, steadfast figure. He has maintained the same weight since he graduated from university, and he was in "first-rate condition" at his last medical exam. These subtle details amplify the sense of tragedy that will unfold, as this healthy, dependable man is killed in an instant.

We also learn he is an intrinsically good, admirable person too. He is the town's "most widely known citizen" despite not being the richest man, which can be seen as a credit to his strength of character as he transcends the typical **paradigm** of the people with the most money having the most esteem and power. He is also described as being "always certain of what he wanted from the world" and having for the most part "obtained it" in the form of his wife Bonnie and their four children. The two eldest daughters have moved out of home, one married with a ten month old baby boy, and the other engaged and studying nursing.

Paradigm: patterns or models of concepts.

Capote then details Mrs Bonnie Clutter's "nervous[ness]" and "little spells" – evidence of her fragile mental state that is a source of "disquiet" in Mr Clutter's life. She has just returned from a psychiatric treatment centre, having been told that her mental health problems may have an underlying physical origin in the form of a pinched nerve in her spine, and as such "sunlight" is "sparkling" on her otherwise "shadowed" condition with the promise of corrective surgery.

This hints at a potential recovery for Mrs Clutter, and the couple experience a happy evening out watching their daughter Nancy in a student theatre performance. This "preview of... normality" is all the more cruel as all four members of the household will be dead a day later.

This leads us to a brief introduction of Nancy, "a real Southern belle" currently dating the "school basketball hero" Bobby Rupp. Nancy is described as "popular and pretty," and although Mr Clutter approves of Bobby's "dependable and gentlemanly" nature, the fact that Bobby is Catholic and the Clutters are Methodists means a long-term relationship is inconceivable. We are also given a verbal tour of the Clutter home, "for the most part designed by Mr Clutter" which further elevates him as the man of the household, establishing literal and familial foundations in Holcomb. It is a "handsome" estate on an "ample" lawn, though it is "similarly furnished" as most other houses would be, which aids Capote's depiction of the Clutters as a normal family who are the victims of such a rare and random tragedy.

And just when you thought you couldn't like Herb Clutter more than we already do, we learn he bakes the best bread in town! Here, Capote conveys the nuances of Mr Clutter's character: he is a "man's man" but he learns to cook out of necessity given his wife's illness. Though Nancy still has a "principal" role in preparing household meals (it is 1959 after all, so gender stereotypes abound!) this detail greatly humanises Mr Clutter.

Furthermore, he "did not smoke, and of course he did not drink; indeed, he had never tasted spirits, and was inclined to avoid people who had." But his **abstinence** does not lead to him being socially **ostracised**, even when he compels his employees and farmhands to adhere to these same principles while on his property, for his generosity of money and of spirit outweighs this. He "paid good wages and distributed frequent bonuses," indicative of his compassion and **magnanimity**.

We then get an overview of the history of the Clutter farm, and we learn that Mr Clutter once "laboured eighteen hour days" in order to establish himself and expand his domain to over 800 acres. In another ominous moment of foreshadowing, Capote describes the property as being "a mile and a half from the highway, and arrived at by obscure roads, it was not a place that strangers came upon by chance." This fact will be what leads to such disbelief and eventually the spreading of rumours in Holcomb after the Clutters are killed, as the general consensus is that their murders cannot have been a crime of circumstance committed by people who stumbled upon their home accidentally. A further **portent** is conveyed through the farm dog, Teddy, who is a "good **sentry**" but is terrified of guns. This culminates in the harrowing line about Mr Clutter "head[ing] for home and the day's work, unaware that it would be his last."

Abstinence: withholding from indulging in something, such as alcohol or sex.

Ostracised: excluded from a society or group.

Magnanimity: generosity and benevolence.

Portent: a sign or warning that a momentous or calamitous event is likely to happen.

Sentry: a soldier set to keep guard over a safe place.

Meeting the Murderers

From here, we shift perspective to Perry and Dick, who we will later learn are the killers. The way Capote draws parallels between Perry and Mr Clutter who both "never drank coffee" creates a morbid connection and implicates them in their respectively tragic fates. He is also a "powerful man," but unlike Mr Clutter, is somewhat disproportionate with a "thick, crouching torso of a weight-lifter" but "stunted legs that seemed grossly inadequate," rendering him simultaneously "overblown and muscle-bound." We learn Perry is an "incessant conceiver of voyages" having travelled the world with "all his worldly belongings: one cardboard suitcase, a guitar, and two boxes of books and maps and songs, poems and old letters." He is also rather complacent; "time rarely weighed upon him, for he had many methods of passing it," again furthering the contrast to Mr Clutter who is out of bed and off to work at precisely 6:30 a.m. Perry's lackadaisical drifter personality is complemented by Dick, who is "practical" and "literal-minded," unable to appreciate Perry's songs and poems about "singing parrots bringing April spring" because, he **laconically** argues, "parrots don't sing." In Perry's eyes, this makes Dick seem "authentically tough, invulnerable" and "totally masculine."

Laconic: using very few words.

Nancy and Friends

We are then transported back to the Clutter's farm where Nancy greets a neighbour on the telephone, Mrs Clarence Katz, who asks if she can bring her daughter Jolene around for Nancy to teach her to bake a cherry pie. This transitions to a more detailed description of Nancy as the golden child – "a straight-A student... president of her class... a skilled rider, an excellent musician," and consistent winner at county fairs for her "pastry, preserves, needlework, flower arrangement," and so on. The **asyndeton** here amplifies the magnitude of Nancy's range of talents. Moreover, she possesses a "radiant jauntiness," and far from being vain about her accomplishments, carries herself with *"character"* that the people of Holcomb regard as having been inherited from her father.

Asyndeton: a list of words without 'and' or 'or' between them.

In yet another indication of the tragic loss of this family from the community, on the day of her death Nancy has already committed to giving trumpet lessons to another neighbour's daughter, and promised to aid her mother in "three complicated errands," as well as attend a meeting with her father. But she compromises with her father and agrees to help Jolene, portraying her as incredibly accommodating and generous, much like Mr Clutter. She is further depicted as an innocent girl with a comfortable routine, brushing her chestnut hair with "a hundred strokes each morning, the same number at night" and eyes that make her "immediately likeable."

Nancy chats to her friend Susan Kidwell on the phone about going to a movie with Bobby the previous night, and **laments** that her father has been expressing his disapproval about the continuation of Nancy and Bobby's relationship despite their differing religious backgrounds.

Lament: a sorrowful or passionate expression of grief.

Sage: profoundly wise.

Still life: a form of painting designed to capture an arrangement of objects.

Ineffable: inexpressible; something too extreme to be expressed in words.

Discordant: something that is not in harmony with its surroundings.

Gewgaw: a useless trinket or ornament.

Florence Nightingale: the founder of modern nursing who cared for soldiers in the 1800s and established practices of hygiene and sanitation in hospitals.

Tenacity: determination, perseverance.

Susan gives some **sage** advice to be happy in the present moment but realistic about the future, though she is limited in her ability to help Nancy navigate the complex emotions of loyalty to her father and affection to her boyfriend. Nancy also relays her concerns about constantly smelling smoke in the house, despite the fact that Mr Clutter does not permit anyone to indulge in cigarettes. Susan astutely picks up on Nancy implying that Mr Clutter himself has been "finding secret solace in tobacco" due to stress.

KEY POINT :
We never find out why Nancy smelled smoke that day. On the surface, this can be read as a symbol of the metaphorical flames that are about the engulf the family and the town, but beyond this, the unanswered question of where the tobacco smoke came from is almost like a distillation of the overarching unanswered question of why this violent crime took place. Perhaps this detail is a reminder of the parts of this story that can never be known.

Meanwhile, Dick and Perry and driving together with a twelve-gauge pump-action shotgun between them. This imagery is described as a "curious **still life**" with an assortment of objects strewn around the Chevrolet, and we are given some more snippets of each man's life story. Perry is apparently "intent on improving his companion's grammar" (casually dropping words like "**ineffable**" into conversation, hinting at his intelligence) and Dick is "twice married, twice divorced." But before we can get a solid vision of these men, we switch back to the Clutters.

Nancy and Jolene have now baked a "blue-ribbon winner" of a pie, and we briefly see Mrs Clutter wander into the scene with a headache. Nancy rushes off to her next commitment, and Mrs Clutter keeps Jolene company while waiting for Mrs Katz to come and collect her. Jolene breaks the ice by relaying how much everyone loves Nancy – their home-economics teacher once said that "Nancy Clutter is always in a hurry, but she always has time. And that's one definition of a lady." This prompts Mrs Clutter to lament that her children are all very efficient and "don't need me." Though this would normally create a rather awkward atmosphere, Mrs Clutter is such a "defenceless person" that Jolene feels relaxed around her, though notes she seems somewhat **discordant** with the rest of the family, as though she is more like a "visiting spinster aunt."

The Tragic Life of Bonnie Clutter

Mrs Clutter begins to ramble so invites Jolene to look at her **gewgaws**, and Capote uses this opportunity to impart on us Bonnie's backstory. She was inspired by **Florence Nightingale** to pursue nursing, though did not have the **tenacity** to cope in a hospital. "Yet to this day she regretted not having completed the course and received her diploma... just to prove... that [she] once succeeded at something." This revelation makes Bonnie the most pitiful of the Clutters, as we are compelled to sympathise with her life's regrets.

She also experienced **postnatal depression** following the birth of each of her children that did not lift after the youngest, Kenyon, was born – "it lingered like a cloud that might rain or might not." Unfortunately, this **exacerbates** her feelings of inadequacy as she is unable to "summon the social vitality" required to bolster the family within Holcomb society. (Perhaps, by implication, Nancy's overachieving tendencies are a subconscious compensation for her mother's struggles.)

Postnatal depression: a condition afflicting mothers after childbirth, typically due to hormonal changes and the psychological adjustment of motherhood.

Nevertheless, Bonnie remains in love with Herb, and her "trust in God sustained her." She tries to delight in the "little things" like her assorted knick-knacks, but her attempts to **ameliorate** her deeper suffering are unsuccessful – she gets a job as a clerk but then feels guilty for enjoying the work too much, and she despairs at the thought of social gatherings and the decision-making they require. Finally, Jolene's mother arrives, and Mrs Clutter bids her farewell with a paper fan as a gift. We then hear more about the darker side of Mrs Clutter's depression, as she is often unable to leave her "austere" bedroom (where she sleeps apart from Herb as he does not want to disturb her with his early rising), and is prone to decision fatigue in Herb's absence. Capote then recounts an experience she had with Susan's mother, Wilma Kidwell, who discovers Mrs Clutter alone in her room one day while the rest of the family are entertaining guests. It is stiflingly hot, so Mrs Kidwell goes to open windows but Mrs Clutter protests "Don't!... I'm not hot. I'm cold. I'm freezing." She then breaks down at the thought of missing out on the events around her, worrying that her family will remember her as "a kind of ghost." All of these devastating details culminate in Capote noting that this is the "final day of her life," and that the Bible on her bedside table contains an embroidered bookmark that reads "Take ye heed, watch and pray: for ye know not when the time is."

Exacerbate: to make a bad thing even worse.

Ameliorate: to lessen the suffering or lighten the burden of someone.

Dick and Perry's Matching Tattoos

Back to Dick and Perry: Capote describes the men as only sharing "surface traits" such as their fastidiousness and good hygiene. We get our first physical description of Dick and his "welterweight" body covered in various "self-designed and self-executed" tattoos (note the meaningful choice of words here; perhaps Capote is foreshadowing that Dick's actions will seal his own fate and death by execution). This "inky gallery" reflects his complicated life, from a blue grinning cat face to a dragon with a human skull in its jaws, to "bosomy nudes" and the word "peace," this hodgepodge makes it difficult for us to form a cohesive picture of who Dick is. He also has some "sentimental concoctions" in the form of flowers dedicated to his parents and his first wife Carol. His facial features consist of "mismatching parts" as a car accident nine years ago left him with a lopsided face. Most tellingly, his eyes are described as "uneven" yet "truly serpentine, with a venomous, sickly-blue squint that although it was involuntarily acquired, seemed nevertheless to warn of bitter sediment at the bottom of his nature." **Analogously**, though Dick's criminality is not something he deliberately sought to cultivate, he nevertheless has a "bitter sediment" as a result of his upbringing and life experiences.

Analogous: similarly, or comparatively.

"But," Perry says, "the eye doesn't matter, Because you have a wonderful smile." Perry likewise was physically scarred from a car accident having had his legs broken in five places, and though he also has tattoos, he instead opted for a 'quality over quantity' approach with more artistic and consistently styled skulls, animals (including a snake that symbolically parallels Dick's "serpentine" eyes), and a floral dedication to a friendly nurse he once knew named Cookie. This mirroring between the two men represents their interconnected trajectories; together they will commit this crime and together they will hang for it. This passage ends with a darkly comic acknowledgement that the "two dudes" seem as though they are on a "double date," though we will soon discover they are heading to seal their fates at the Clutter estate.

More About Holcomb and a Prelude to Murder

Capote then recounts more history of Holcomb and the nearest major town, Garden City, "just another fair-sized town in the middle – almost the exact middle – of the continental United States." Though its inhabitants proudly maintain it is uniquely friendly and picturesque (and not at all racist or classist!), Capote presents it as an epitome of a normal American county, with its supposedly distinctive features and hyperbolic claims like "World's Largest FREE Swimpool" only compounding this sense of a relatable small town. But we are told Mr Clutter does not seek to climb his way up to the **echelons** of the Garden City Country Club, preferring instead to take part in Holcomb's modest "golfing foursome" and the "4-H Club... 'Head, Heart, Hands, Health'," which adds to our portrait of his rural identity and generosity. Nancy and Kenyon are also members, who join their father in helping those living in remote areas in ways that develop their "practical abilities and moral character." The latter is evident in the anecdote about Herb announcing an Achievement Banquet dedicated to Mrs Ashida, a Japanese woman relatively new to the town who has herself contributed to the 4-H Club, and who walks for miles to deliver soup to anyone in Holcomb who is sick. Mrs Ashida expresses her gratitude to Mr Clutter, and recalls the bountiful gifts of produce that she had not yet planted on their farm when they first arrived. She and her husband Hideo consider it "the best place we've ever lived," and though they are contemplating moving away to another farm in Nebraska, Mr Clutter tries to convince them to stay. This otherwise happy recollection ends with yet another eerie line about how Mrs Ashida's respect for Mr Clutter's "self-assurance" and the fact that she "cannot imagine [him] afraid. No matter what happened, you'd talk your way out of it."

Echelon: the tiers or ranks in society.

Dick and Perry attempt to buy material for their 'heist,' though Dick insists they don't need stockings to disguise their faces because there will be "*no* witnesses." Though he intends this to mean they will rob the Clutter house without being seen, this prophecy does indeed come true as the men kill all four Clutters that witnessed them being there.

Nevertheless, Dick is overly confident in his "flawlessly devised" plan, though this is rapidly unravelled when Perry asks the basic question of how much rope they would need to tie up an unknown amount of people who may be in the house. They purchase an excessive amount of rope, but this **belies** how under-prepared they are to carry out this attempted larceny.

Belie: to give a false or misleading impression.

Kenyon and Friend

The final member of the Clutter household we are introduced to is Kenyon. Six feet tall and resembling neither of his parents, he is "cursed with a lanky boy's lack of muscular coordination" and poor eyesight. He still plays team sports, though only tokenistically, and has only one friend (Bob Jones, who lives on a neighbouring ranch) with whom he regularly goes rabbit hunting. Unfortunately Bob fails to put bros before... his new girlfriend, and this causes a rift between him and Kenyon. This portrait of the Clutters only son, especially when juxtaposed with the perfectionist Nancy, explores the vulnerability of a boy on the cusp of manhood who has not yet settled into a stereotypically masculine identity. Though he is a good shot with a gun, an undoubtedly revered talent in Kansas, he ultimately "lives in a world of his own."

Kenyon and the housekeeper's husband, Mr Helm, observe an insurance agent coming to meet with Mr Clutter. Kenyon and Nancy lightly tease each other before Mr Helm departs, with Capote noting he would later testify "that... was the last I seen them... nothing out of the ordinary."

Willie-Jay's Letter

Dick and Perry are still fighting over whether to bring stockings to disguise themselves, with Dick winning out and stopping the car to go purchase them. Perry is left to reflect on his own superstitious nature and belief in fate, eventually letting his thoughts wander to his friendship with Willie-Jay while incarcerated at the Kansas State Penitentiary. Willie-Jay was the chaplain's clerk and sings in the prison choir with a glorious **tenor** voice, and he attempts to bring Perry "to God" despite Perry's "never very earnest spiritual quest." He is released from jail before Pery, but writes him a farewell letter that ends by calling Perry a "man of extreme passion... striving to project [his] individuality against a backdrop of rigid conformity." In his words, Perry is "strong, but there is a flaw in [his] strength" in the form of his predisposition towards "explosive emotional reaction[s]." This letter is **laden** with potent foreshadowing, but also startlingly **incisive** insights into Perry's character, "despis[ing]" people because he **erroneously** believes "their happiness is the source" of his "frustration and resentment," when in fact it is his own internal destructive tendencies that wreak havoc on his life. Dick dismisses all of this as "hooey" and the work of a "faggot," and Perry revels in the "counterbalance" that Dick represents as a "shrewd... realist" who would never criticise Perry as Willie-Jay does.

Tenor: the highest singing range for a typical male.

Laden: heavily loaded or weighed down.

Incisive: sharp, penetrating, and insightful.

Erroneously: falsely.

Willie-Jay's moral judgement "haunt[s] the hallways of [Perry's] mind," with pensive insights like "you pursue the negative" echoing in Perry's conscience. However, Perry's belief in fate leads him astray, as Willie-Jay's release from prison coincides with him forming the plot with Dick. He makes an effort to locate Willie-Jay after he serves his own time, but is told by the chaplain that he has ventured elsewhere to find "a decent job," leaving Perry "dizzy with anger and disappointment," as Willie-Jay was the only one to recognise his "worth." This is also the first hint at Perry's desperate search for a male role model or some kind of guiding force. Dick interrupts this reverie, and they continue on.

Herb's Life Insurance

Mr Clutter meets with insurance representative Bob Johnson, and we learn (contrary to rumours going around in prison) that Herb is a man who "never carry[s] cash." He laments that Kenyon isn't a "born rancher" with the ability to take over when his father dies, though there is some solace in the fact that his eldest children have married stable men who will take care of them. Johnson remarks that Mr Clutter is too concerned with his own **mortality** given that he is a healthy 48 year old, joking that "we're likely to have you around a couple weeks more" (real funny, Bob). Compounding the **dramatic irony** of the situation, Mr Clutter is "optimistic" about his future, though he has just hours to live. That he signs this insurance policy on the day of his death is an almost implausible coincidence, but ultimately adds to the text's examination of life's chaotic and **aleatory** nature.

Mortality: being capable of dying, or aware that you will die one day.

Dramatic irony: when the audience is aware of something and the characters are not.

Aleatory: completely random; depending on the roll of a dice.

Meanwhile, Perry sings a religious ballad with his guitar (the capitalisation of "He" typically refers to God) to remind us of his history with Willie-Jay. He hates the "flat and limitless" landscape that feels "empty and lonesome to him" – already this conflicts with our understanding of the warmth and hospitality of the Clutters and Holcomb, and perhaps suggests Perry is too emotionally stunted to appreciate what Holcomb has to offer. This passage ends with Perry singing and a full moon rising before we jump forward a few days later.

Bobby Rupp's Testimony

Technically this part of the chapter continues on from the "full moon" where we left off, but Capote precedes this by noting it is now the following Monday and Bobby Rupp is giving evidence prior to taking a lie detector test, thereby confirming something drastic has occurred in the interim. Bobby explains that he phoned Nancy at around 6:50 p.m. and remembers Nancy fondly as a girl who "made everybody feel good about themselves" as well as her father Mr Clutter who "never tried to make you feel he was right and you were wrong." Much of this section are direct excerpts of Bobby's testimony, arriving at the house shortly after seven to spend time with Nancy. His recount includes many precise details about what Nancy was wearing, why Mr Clutter ate two apples, and what was on television. He also reaffirms how much the family love each other, and how Nancy was fond of Kenyon even though no one "exactly understood him."

Bobby leaves at around 10:30, making arrangements for a movie date with Nancy the next day, and when he thinks back, he reflects that someone "must have been hiding... among the trees."

Dick and Perry Approach

Dick and Perry stop for a lavish dinner before driving to Garden City, proudly labelled "A Friendly Place" by signs outside of town. They also stop for petrol, and Perry discovers a tear in his gloves that he considers a bad omen. The petrol attendant, James Spor, makes small talk with Dick by asking if he is "here to hunt" to which Dick replies that they are "just passing through." We get more of a glimpse into Dick's mindset here, and Dick's high esteem of Perry being "a natural killer – absolutely sane, but conscienceless and capable of dealing, with or without motive, the coldest-blooded deathblows." He had apparently committed to "woo[ing]" Perry so that he could profit from this "gift," though he comes to find Perry may just be an "ordinary punk."

Nancy's Last Evening

The building tensions collide with the descriptions of Nancy's innocent, child-like bedroom, replete with a teddy bear Bobby won for her at a fair, and a cork board with photos of her friends and family. She is the last to go to bed, indulging in a night-time beauty routine and laying out her church clothes for the next morning, which Capote signals will be the "dress in which she was to be buried." Capote then includes some quotes from Nancy's final diary entry that night: mostly quotidian events with occasional teenage outbursts about her love for Bobby. She has kept this diary for over four years, though consciously changes her handwriting throughout as she gradually forms a **nascent,** adolescent identity.

Gruesome Discovery

Nancy Clutter's friend Nancy Ewalt and her father Mr Clarence Ewalt arrive at the Clutter farm on Sunday morning, as the Clutters typically took Nancy Ewalt to church with them. She rings the doorbell to no avail so she and her father head to the school (or "Teacherage" – the living quarters for teaching staff) to find Susan and Mrs Kidwell. Nancy and Susan remark that it is highly unlikely the Clutters would still be sleeping, and as we're told Susan later recounted in "a statement made at a later date" (more foreshadowing!) when she called their home phone it rang out after a minute. When they go back to the house together, Susan describes the **incongruously** "too bright and quiet" atmosphere, and she notes how many things seemed out of place. Nancy Ewalt and Susan are the ones to first discover what has happened when Susan goes upstairs to Nancy's room which was "full of sunlight." She states that she does not remember screaming, just that she remembers "Nancy's Teddy bear staring at me. And Nancy." This is a powerful **omission** of detail; Capote does not revel in the gore or the horror – instead, we see this loss through the eyes of a friend who is clearly struggling to articulate the confronting scene she stumbled upon.

Nascent: something that is still developing and has only just started coming into existence.

Incongruous: not in keeping with something's normal environment.

Omission: not including something.

Mr Ewalt hears his daughter's distress and is told Nancy Clutter is dead. He picks up the Clutter's phone to call the police but sees the line has been cut. This is a clear indication of foul play, and a sinister symbol for what transpired in the Clutter house that left them unable to call for help.

We are then introduced to Larry Hendricks, English teacher and part-time school bus driver, who we will stay with for several pages as he discovers the bodies of all four Clutters. He overhears Susan and Nancy Ewalt when Mr Ewalt brings them back to the Teacherage in their hysterical states. Hendricks notes "Susan never has got over it. Never will, ask me." This tense implies Hendricks is speaking long after the events of that day, which amplifies the sense of trauma the two girls endured. Hendricks overhears Mr Ewalt call the sheriff to tell him there is "something *radically* wrong" at the Clutters', and then the two men accompany the sheriff to the property. Hendricks recalls telling himself to "make a note of every detail. In case I was ever called on to testify in court."

At 9:35 a.m. the sheriff arrives and quickly calls for "reinforcements and an ambulance" as "there's been some kind of accident." Though Susan and Nancy's reactions were undoubtedly emotionally hysterical, here we see a professional officer of the law unable to come to terms with what has happened. Upon discovering Nancy Clutter's body, Henricks states "it was pretty bad" (you'd think an English teacher would be a bit more descriptive...) and it is here that we finally get a sense of the tragedy that has happened. She has been "shot in the back of the head with a shotgun held maybe two inches away... the wall was covered with blood" and her hands and ankles were bound behind her, though with a Venetian blind cord instead of a rope, suggesting some degree of improvisation rather than **premeditation**.

Premeditation: to intentionally plan out one's actions (or more often a crime) beforehand.

They check Kenyon's room and find nothing, so they go to Mrs Clutter's room and find her body tied with her hands in front of her instead – an inconsistency that further contradicts the idea of a carefully planned attack – and she looks as though she is praying. She has also been elaborately tied to the footboard of her bed, and is wearing jewellery which is "one of the reasons why [Hendricks] always discounted robbery as a motive." Her mouth is taped up, but the impact of the bullet shot to the side of her head had ripped it loose. "Her eyes were open. Wide open. As though she were still looking at the killer. Because she must have had to watch him do it – aim the gun." The men are too stunned to speak, but they continue to search the house with Hendricks noting as they checked Mr Clutter's room that "he never did carry any cash." There are further indications that things are amiss – Mr Clutter's glasses are on a bureau even though he cannot see without them, and there are no signs of a struggle anywhere. The sheriff checks the Clutters' guns and determines they have not been fired recently, so they venture into the basement.

There, they find Kenyon's body, the one that "haunts [Hendricks] the most" because he "looked the most like himself," despite the fact that he had been shot in the face. They also find Mr Clutter's body covered in more blood than there should have been in a "plain shooting," for his throat had been cut, and he had at one point had his hands tied by a cord to a pipe on the ceiling. "But why? To torture him? I don't guess we'll ever know." The fact that Hendricks' memories of that day are **interpolated** with his present tense thoughts and reflections only deepens the mysteries that unfold. Moreover, now that this whole chapter of dramatic irony and foreshadowing is now coming to fruition, Capote begins to plant the seeds of questions like "why" which he will explore in subsequent chapters.

Interpolated: inserting something of a different nature in amongst something else.

Ambulances, photographers, the coroner, and a priest soon arrive, along with other people from town having come straight from church and treating the scene with a similar quiet reverence. The **undersheriff,** Wendle Meier, talks to Alfred Stoecklein who was Mr Clutter's closest neighbour and was caring for his sick baby all night, though he and his wife did not hear anything after the sound of Bobby Rupp's car leaving. As Hendricks leaves, he sees Kenyon's dog Teddy in a state of shock with its tail between its legs, and this traumatic passage ends with the stilted lines "I'd been too dazed, too numb, to feel the full viciousness of it. The suffering. The horror. They were dead. A whole family. Gentle, kindly people, people *I* knew – *murdered.* You had to believe it, because it was really true."

Undersheriff: a deputy sheriff.

The Aftermath in Holcomb

Capote transitions away from this to the perspective of Mrs Sadie 'Mother' Truitt, the mail messenger. She is a 75 year old woman and the oldest native-born resident, and her daughter Mrs Myrtle Clare now works as the local postmistress. The post office is just as dilapidated as the rest of town: "the ceiling leaks, the floorboards wobble, the mailboxes won't shut, the light bulbs are broken, the clock has stopped." But according to Mother Truitt, "the stamps work," which conveys her optimism amidst her circumstances, which she regards as "cosy," replete with a rocking chair, coffee, and plenty of reading material.

Mother Truitt recalls seeing two ambulances drive past on Sunday morning and discussing this with her daughter. Myrtle postulates that these are likely for Bonnie, given her **interminable** health problems, but Mother Truitt questions why there would be *two* ambulances for one person. Myrtle then calls Mabel Helm, the Clutters' housekeeper, who informs her that all four Clutters are dead. The two theorise about who could have shot them before Myrtle concludes it does not matter how one dies, for "it's all the same in eternity."

Interminable: seemingly never-ending.

The Garden City radio station broadcasts news of the "unbelievable and shocking beyond words" tragedy, causing a "shallow horror sensation" to ripple across Holcomb "that cold springs of personal fear swiftly deepened." The owner of Hartman's Cafè Mrs Bess Hartman offers her own theories and summarises some town gossip about the killings; the **high modality** in her declaration that "it must have been a grudge" has additional layers of dramatic irony for readers who know the reality of the case. She also laments that the "worst part of the crime" is that neighbours "can't look at each other without kind of wondering," and that the identity of the murderers would be "a bigger surprise than the murders themselves."

High modality: using definitive language that implies absolute certainty.

The insurance agent Bob Johnson who met with Herb Clutter the day before he died receives a phone call informing him of the news just as he is settling down to Sunday dinner with his wife – another instance of tragedy interrupting otherwise normal, **quotidian** events. He ponders the incredibly coincidental timing of Mr Clutter's new insurance policy, and although legally his company was not obliged to pay out the insurance to his two surviving daughters, he decides to do the "moral thing" and follow through. Eveanna and Beverley are informed of the day's events, as are the various other next of kin in the Clutter family, and funeral arrangements are made.

Quotidian: daily routine or regular occurrences.

Bobby Rupp hears the news from Mr Ewalt and enters into a slightly catatonic state until he decides to walk to the Clutter farm where he meets with Susan Kidwell and he cries with her, though not before Capote remarks that "Bobby, as he was to learn before nightfall, was [the] principal suspect."

Finally, we rejoin Perry is in a "far off" hotel room. The only clue that he is involved in what has transpired is that he is washing his boots in "vaguely pink-tinted water" (implying they still have some of the Clutters' blood on them). Dick has returned to his family home for a Sunday dinner, "kiss[ing] his mother" and conversing with his father as though everything was normal, even though he had "among other things, driven over eight hundred miles in the past twenty-four hours." These veiled references to the "other things" and Capote's **lacuna** in the actual acts of murder end this passage with an unsatisfying lack of clarity – the same sensation that he attempts to capture amongst those in Holcomb.

Lacuna: a gap or unfilled space.

This concludes the first chapter.

Persons Unknown

The Investigation Begins

Chapter 2 opens with Mr Clutter's hunting companions making the "familiar journey" to the farm in an "unfamiliar spirit," having volunteered to clean the house after the bloody murders by, for now, "persons unknown." They make their way through the home and eventually take the unsalvageable contents to light a bonfire, with Mr Clutter's friend of thirty years Andy Erhard questioning "how it was possible that such effort, such plain virtue, could overnight be reduced to this – smoke, thinning as it rose and was received by the big, annihilating sky."

We then meet the Kansas Bureau of Investigation (KBI) and our hero Alvin Dewey who will lead the investigation in this "apparently motiveless, all but clueless" crime, and won't rest until he finds out "the why and the who." Having known the Clutters personally, he heads up the team of the "ablest investigators" and establishes himself as a highly fact-driven, logical operator with two possible theories: "a single-killer concept and a double-killer concept," playing out potential scenarios in his mind, though he acknowledges the flaws in these prevailing models as "if Herb had thought his family was in danger, mortal danger, he would have fought like a tiger" and was presumably physically adept enough to overpower one man, or even two. From the start, Dewey is troubled by the case; the idea of someone with an "insane grudge... doesn't make sense. But then, come right down to it, nothing does."

Dewey reads Nancy's diary, and although Bobby is still a suspect at this point, Dewey does not think he is involved. The youngest detective, Harold Nye, interviews the remaining members of the Clutter family, but all he learns is that "of all the people in all the world, the Clutters were the least likely to be murdered." We also meet the other members of the KBI team, Roy Church and Clarence Duntz, as they pursue some leads, as well as Dewey's wife Marie whose newfound concerns about the safety of Holcomb are evident in her having changed all the locks on their house. Many in Holcomb now leave their lights on all night, some unable to sleep for fear that "it might happen again,' for to them, the unexpected crime is akin to "being told there is no God. It makes life seem pointless."

Clues are Few

There is a bitter juxtaposition in Arthur Clutter, Herb's brother, postulating that "whoever did it was someone within ten miles of where we now stand," and Capote's transition to Dick and Perry that begins with "approximately four hundred miles east of where Arthur Clutter then stood." The two murderers are in a dinner reveling over news headlines about how the search is on for the "killers whose... cunning is apparent if his (or their) motive is not." Perry finds it hard to believe there are no leads, but to Dick, this is proof that the crime was expertly executed.

Perry recounts the story of his brother's death – a man enamoured with his wife but driven mad by jealous suspicion, shooting her out of fear that she was cheating on him, and then shooting himself the next day. Perry claims that for both this event and his own motorbike accident, he had "a premonition" that something terrible would happen. He describes a recurring dream about being swallowed by a snake, as well as a motif of a yellow bird who Perry hallucinates saving him as his "hovering avenger" when he is being abused by nuns. This is our first glimpse into the tumultuous childhood of a "hated, hating half-breed child" who, among other things, was frequently beaten for wetting the bed. By contrast, Dick simply announces "I'm a normal," though the similarities and differences between the men will continue to unfold as the novel progresses.

Susan's Aftermath and Dick's Cheque Ruse

Susan relays her fondness for Nancy Clutter, practically a "sister," and how she and Bobby would reminisce about her together after the funeral. She dismisses the theory of a "hired killer" as "just gossip... everything Nancy despised," and states that she herself doesn't particularly care who the killer was, for her "friend is gone. Knowing who killed her isn't going to bring her back." She also recalls the red velvet Nancy was dressed in for the funeral, but that it had to be a closed-casket ceremony because of the "disquieting" effect of the bodies having their heads wrapped in white cotton to conceal the damage done by the shotgun.

Perry reads about this funeral in a newspaper, impressed by the thousand people that attend, before being roped into Dick's plan to pass fake cheques in order to fund their next journey. Dick constructs an elaborate lie to convince a clerk in a clothing store that he is a wealthy man buying clothing for an upcoming wedding. (The ploy is that Dick seems so trustworthy and rich that a shop owner will allow him to pay for something via a cheque instead of cash, and he'll add a hundred dollars on top of the bill so he walks out with that cash and a promise to pay everything in full later.) But while Dick effortlessly constructs a narrative about Perry getting married just so he can 'buy' a diamond ring by cheque and then pawn it minutes later, Perry gets invested in the "make-believe bride," and adds emotional detail to the story in his mind.

Perry's thoughts wander to the girl he "almost married" – a nurse named Cookie who cared for him while he was recovering from his accident. She developed feelings for him, but he abandons her with some lines by the English poet Robert W Service that Perry claims to have written himself. The poem is fittingly titled *The Men That Don't Fit In*, and describes a personality type that "can't stay still" and desires the "strange and new." He credits Cookie for helping him appreciate "serious literature," despite his lack of formal education, and this is something that will recur throughout the text.

Dewey's Life and Beverly's Wedding

Meanwhile, Dewey is receiving incessant phone calls from journalists requesting information, conspiracy theorists suggesting their own, or drunken idiots confessing to the crime themselves, but he answers every one, hoping that it will be "the break that brings down the curtain." So far, Nye has concluded their leads have added up to "a nice round number. Zero," save for the fact that the housekeeper Mrs Helm noted that Kenyon's radio was missing. Dewey is further troubled by the realisation that all four victims seem to have been made "comfortable" in death using pillows or bedcovers, but he has yet to find "the link" that will help him understand it all, consoling his wife that things will "get back to normal" one day, though he is interrupted yet again by the telephone.

Beverly Clutter marries her fiancé Vere English on November 23rd since all of her relatives are in Holcomb for the funeral anyway. After their departure, Mrs Bonnie Clutter's brother Howard writes an editorial thanking the town for welcoming them in such difficult circumstances, but pleads with them to not desire retribution or "hold a grudge in our hearts" against "the doer of this act." This more forgiving attitude towards wrongdoers is also something that we will see repeatedly as the novel progresses.

Dick and Perry's Picnic and Journey to Mexico

Perry remarks that there "must be something wrong with" the two of them to have committed the murders, but Dick refuses to engage, "annoyed as hell" by the discussion and wishing that Perry would "shut up," though upon reflection, he does think to himself that there is something wrong with Perry, recalling the prison stories of him bedwetting, crying for his Dad in his sleep, and also possessing a **volatile** "inward rage." Ironically though, Dick can acknowledge Perry should scare him, but is himself too psychologically damaged to feel fear. As a further demonstration of his psychopathy, Dick then runs over a dog with their car.

Volatile: liable to change rapidly and unpredictably.

We then see this same conversation from Perry's perspective; he feels "spells of helplessness" about that night, unable to prevent his mind from reliving the memories of "a silver dollar rolling across a floor... the hysterical inhalations of a man with a severed windpipe." He also ponders whether his personality is not his fault, and considers the fates of his family: his alcoholic mother choked to death, his sister Fern jumped out of a window (though Perry "tried to believe she slipped" because he was fond of her artistic, dancing, singing soul), and his brother Jimmy shot his wife and then himself. Only his eldest sister Barbara had escaped to raise a family, though we later learn Perry cannot establish a healthy relationship with her. He also recalls his murder of "the nigger" that Dick heard about – a **transient** named King whom Perry supposedly murdered with a bicycle chain without feeling anything afterwards, though Perry reveals this was a complete fabrication (beyond the fact that Perry once met a black man named King).

Transient: a homeless person or drifter who only stays in a place for a short time.

The "rumourmongers" in Holcomb have now latched onto the "Jones Theory" which postulates that the Clutter's neighbour Taylor Jones was the intended target of the crime, as he is a far richer man. Meanwhile, Mrs Ashida and her family have committed to moving to Nebraska, unable to get over the tragic death of Mr Clutter, though she notes that he was probably unafraid until the end, believing like most of the town did that nothing like this could ever happen to him.

Dick and Perry spend a week in Mexico City before venturing further south with a vagabond named Otto, meandering around while Dick is "accosted" by prostitutes he sleeps with and frequently proposes to marry. Otto does some sketches of the two men, and they all go fishing together. These snippets of their attempts at a carefree life are deliberately interspersed with the emotional recollections of the people of Holcomb reeling in the wake of the crime, as well as insights from the detectives struggling to piece together the mystery.

Mr Paul Helm fondly remembers his former employer, though is troubled by the fact that the police do not believe his sudden recollection of a pair of Mexicans who visited the Clutter farm looking for work the day before they died. He also contemplates the loss of Bonnie who would often watch the family from her bedroom window, "a ghost behind the glass," but when he looks up at the house, he squints in the sunlight but thinks he sees someone inside. Not believing in "spook[s]," he calls the sheriff, and they discover a drifter named Jonathan Adrian who was curious to see what was inside the house and snuck in through a pipe into the basement. However, Adrian is promptly arrested when Dewey and the team discover a shotgun and hunting knife in his car.

A History of My Boy's Life by Tex Smith

Back in Mexico City, Dick has sold the car and they're run out of money, but Perry feels unable to leave Dick due to his attachment issues, though he attributes this to his superstitious belief that they won't be apprehended if they stick together. His guitar has been stolen but without a car he is unable to travel with his books and other belongings, so he tries to mail them to himself in Nevada so he can pick them up later. One of the things he keeps, though, is a manuscript written by his father in an effort to help Perry be granted parole, entitled "A History of My Boy's Life." This is where the many traumas of Perry's youth come to light. His father recounts his healthy birth, but a struggle with his "disgraceful drunkard" of a mother. Custody battles ensue with Perry seeking to run away with his father, and eventually his father takes Perry with him while his siblings are placed in homes. Perry was also involved in many school fights, apparently only when bullies picked on him, and though his father defends him, he eventually decides to pull Perry out of school altogether. Perry later joins the Marines but gives up after he breaks both legs and his hip in a motorcycle accident. He does his best to paint his son in a positive light, describing him as being "goodhearted if you treat him rite." This manuscript is riddled with spelling mistakes and poor grammar and punctuation, as Perry's father is not an educated man, though considers himself and Perry "self taught" men.

Perry's "biography always set racing a stable of emotions" within him, including "self-pity... love and hate" with hate ultimately winning out. He recalls a "not... unhappy existence" when his parents worked as professional rodeo performers before they fought and divorced. Perry's mother allows liquor to "sour her soul" and "dissolve her self-respect" until she begins to prostitute herself out to men whose names she does not know, and Perry ended up in a Catholic orphanage with abusive nuns he calls "Black Widows." He contracts pneumonia after a nun tries to drown him in ice-cold water, at which point his father rescues him and takes him to live a nomadic lifestyle. He recalls with resentment that he had some artistic talents, but "never got any encouragement – from [his father] or anybody else." After his motorcycle accident, he spent time with an Indian logger named Joe James who helps nurse Perry back to health, and though Joe and Perry are only two years apart, Joe treats him like one of his children, teaching him how to read.

After this, Perry reunites with his father, though their attempt to open a hunting lodge in Alaska fails to attract any interest or money, leaving them "downright hungry" and tense. This culminates in a fight over a biscuit that ends with Perry attempting to strangle him, and then his father pulling the trigger on a gun to shoot him saying "Look at me, Perry. I'm the last living thing you're ever gonna see." But the gun is not loaded, and his father collapses in tears. After this, his father locks him out of the house and casts his belongings out into the snow, abandoning Perry once again. He hitchhikes his way to Kansas where he meets Dick, and he is later arrested when a police officer pulls him over for speeding and discovers stolen goods in his car.

The other letter Perry has in his possession is one written by his sister Barbara to him while he was in prison, which is markedly different in tone. She tells him about her three children, Freddie, Baby, and Donnie, and how far her life has come, before expressing her moral philosophy that "none of us have *anyone* to blame for *whatever* we have done with our own personal lives," as after the age of seven, people are thought to have reached "the age of reason" where one understands the difference between right and wrong. Though this is somewhat reductive, and does not account for the role a traumatic childhood can play in compromising one's cognitive development during critical periods, but nevertheless Barbara is a stark example of how things could have turned out differently for Perry had he made better choices. It seems she has come to terms with her childhood in a much healthier way, and is now a well-adjusted adult who considers it "no shame to have a dirty face" or traumatic past, but that "the same comes when you *keep* it dirty" and do nothing to better one's life. She pleads with him to take more responsibility and stop blaming his father for his own deeds, for he is "a human being with a *free will,*" but this fails to reach Perry, who remarks that he "loathed" Barbara and cruelly tells Dick he wished she were one of the Clutters that they murdered.

The only reason he keeps this is because Willie-Jay wrote notes entitled "Impressions I Garnered From the Letter" which calls it "foolish... born of human failing." He critiques Barbara's hypocrisy in attempting to demonstrate Christian principles, arguing "it is easy to ignore the rain if you have a raincoat," and he advises Perry not to communicate with her any further.

Though this may have been well-intentioned, Willie-Jay inadvertently validates the same "dangerous anti-social instincts" that he will later criticise Perry for in his own letter. Aside from these letters, his only other remaining possessions are his Bronze Star from the army, the high school diploma he earned while incarcerated, his diary, and his dictionary of words "worth memorising," which explains his penchant for fancy words.

Anyway, Dick has been having the opposite of wholesome family remembrances, as he is having sex with a prostitute named Inez next door, who is yet another woman that believes Dick's promises of marriage though they are leaving Mexico that afternoon. It is important to consider the disparity in how Capote treats the two men here, and the time he dedicates to exploring Perry's **fraught** life compared to the cursory references to Dick that render him less relatable and human.

Fraught: a situation filled with or likely to result in something undesirable.

Dewey Returns to the Clutter Home

People in Holcomb worry that Dewey has not made much progress on the Clutter case, his dedication to the puzzle resulting in "uncharacteristic absent-mindedness" and him losing about ten kilos from stress, as though he was an "**ascetic** absorbed in occult pursuits," suggesting a complete dedication and immersion in his work. We learn that Adrian is no longer a suspect, and we get a brief overview of Holcomb's crime history and the few murders that have occurred there in the past fifty years, though Dewey considers these "**squalls** preceding a hurricane." He visits the "peaceful" Clutter home as he has done many times, labouring under the assumption that the Clutters must have known "the persons who destroyed them," but this does not trigger any revelations in him. When he returns home, his wife mentions he had a dream about Bonnie Clutter who is deeply unhappy in death. Marie Dewey tries to comfort her, but Bonnie murmurs "To be murdered. No. No. There's nothing worse. Nothing worse than that. Nothing."

Ascetic: a person who deliberately deprives themselves of a comfortable lifestyle.

Squall: a gust of wind.

The chapter ends with Dick and Perry hitchhiking back to America, Perry singing "hallelujah" on his harmonica as he goes.

Answer

The Murder Weapon

Chapter 3 opens on Floyd Wells a prisoner who "not only... kn[e]w the murdered family, [but] who murdered them." He was a former employee of Mr Clutter, and thinks on him and the whole "nice family" fondly. However, he mistakenly partakes in habitual prison bragging and constructs a lie about Mr Clutter keeping thousands of dollars in his safe, and this inspires Dick to concoct a plan to "tie them people up and gun them down," though Floyd doesn't believe he will ever go through with this. After it happens, he confesses to another prisoner and ultimately feels it is his duty to Herb Clutter – who had "never done [him] no harm" and had even given him a Christmas present of fifty dollars – to inform the authorities. Word of this information reaches Dewey, who is then able to find mugshots and profiles of Dick and Perry, which he shows his wife

Agent Nye visits Dick's father, Mr Hicock, who proclaims that there was "nothing wrong with [his] boy" until he "concussed his head in a car smash-up. After that he wasn't the same boy." Again, this contrasts greatly with the protracted sufferings of Perry's childhood that Capote dedicates several pages to. Ultimately, Mr Hickock is at a loss as to his son's actions, though his tearful wife blames "that friend of his," meaning Perry. Nye also interviews various other neighbours and acquaintances who describe his family as "fine people" but Dick an **amoral** man who wouldn't hesitate to steal from a dead man. When Nye returns to the Hickock home to ask about Dick visiting shortly after the murders, his "trained eyes" spy a shotgun that he is "certain" was the weapon that was used to kill the Clutters. But not wanting to arouse suspicion, Nye leaves, and Mr Hickock affirms that while Dick is "ashamed" of his actions, they have an unconditional love for him as his parents.

Amoral: completely without morals, or existing without any concern for morality (in contrast to 'immorality,' which means having bad morals).

There are also a brief scenes of Dick and Perry still hitchhiking, and they come close to killing a man who offers them a lift before he pulls over to pick up another drifter. Later, they shelter from the rain just over the Iowa border on their way back to Kansas, as Dick wants to continue his fake cheque ploy there. Perry warns him they could end up in "The Corner," a colloquial term for Kansas State Penitentiary's death row (and given that serves as the name of Chapter 4, we can deduce this premonition will come true).

Barbara's Memories and Back in Kansas

Back to Nye: there is now a manhunt for Dick and Perry, and they discover Perry's box of belongings he had mailed to himself – there are few useful clues, but Nye still appreciates it for giving him "a clearer impression of the owner and his lonely, mean life." He sets out to interview Tex Smith, Perry's father, and learns Perry had been looking for him recently.

Eventually, he finds Barbara who explains Perry's life story to Nye, and that she has always been "afraid of [Perry]... he can *seem* so warm-hearted and sympathetic... oh, he can fool you. He can make you feel so sorry for him." Capote also wonders whether what Barbara is truly afraid of is the Smith family curse and the "terrible destinies" that had befallen her siblings. We get another glimpse into her mindset and her "ambivalent... respect" for her father, though she considers such men should live "alone" as opposed to with wives and children. She also reveals her contempt for Perry's insistence that their father was the one who stifled Perry's entire life – "Oh the man I could have been! But that bastard never gave me a chance." – and when Nye leaves, she "bolted the door" to keep out both the "dead as well as the living," indicating her desperation to escape from a past that never leaves her mind.

Dewey, meanwhile, is being careful not to assume Dick and Perry are guilty, and he knows the case lacks any substantial evidence he could use to catch them out in lies if they refused to confess. He is also struggling to reconcile the fact that these men seemingly killed four people just to steal a child's radio, thinking it "inconceivable" that they would have done so after failing to find the money-filled safe. In town, people are still talking, and Myrtle Clare expresses her somewhat nihilistic world view that "you live until you die, and it doesn't matter *how* you go."

By now, Dick and Perry are back in Kansas in a laundromat, though Perry is worried with "**apprehension**," lamenting that he was "still (and wasn't it incredible, a person of his intelligence, his talents?) an urchin dependent, so to say, on stolen coins." This **self-reproach** now takes on a slightly different meaning as we have heard Barbara's perspective of Perry's **penchant** for blaming his misfortunes on others and failing to take any personal responsibilities.

Apprehension: anxiety or fear that something bad will happen.

Self-reproach: blame directed at oneself.

Penchant: tendency or inclination towards.

Perhaps influenced by his wife's dream of Mrs Clutter, Agent Dewey dreams about having dinner with Mr Clutter and his presumed killers, Dick and Perry. He chases them to a graveyard and wonders if his father's tombstone is nearby, when he sees the murderers standing by the mass grave of the Clutters. Dewey tries to shoot them, but the bullets are ineffective and the men become transparent and evaporate, laughing as they do. This is a highly symbolic dream, representing Dewey's frustrations in pursuing "phantoms" that he at times considers "invulnerable," and having to implicitly confront his own mortality, or the deaths of his own family. He wakes to news that Dick and Perry are in Kansas with a stolen car and stolen license plates, as Nye has followed Dick's path of fake cheques through the state.

Christmas

However, Dick and Perry manage to flee in time to Miami Beach in Florida, where Perry is pestering his companion with stories of other murders in the news. While on a beach, it is revealed that Dick harbours a "sexual interest in female children" and has "seduc[ed] pubescent girls... eight or nine times in the last several years." He attempts to do the same to a twelve year old girl on the beach to no avail, and Perry watches with revulsion, having "no respect for people who can't control themselves sexually," especially when it came to "pevertiness" in people like Dick. This compounds Capote's portrayal of Perry as a sympathetic man and Dick as an inherently unsympathetic one, and is also a moment where Perry hints at his role at having prevented Dick from raping Nancy Clutter.

Although Perry appreciates the Christmas carols and cathedral choir's "exalted music," he finds himself contemplating suicide as a seeming inevitable "specific death awaiting him," whilst Dick has no such qualms, enjoying the "wonderful" ocean water.

From here we switch perspectives to Bobby Rupp who is struggling to get through Christmas, a date that was so close to Nancy Clutter's birthday. He used to find it challenging to think of "two suitable gifts in such quick succession... but then Nancy had died." He feels as though his grief has "drawn a circle around him he could not escape from and others could not enter," though does feel an affinity towards Susan Kidwell who shares in his loss Nancy, though even they gradually drift apart as while in one another's company they cannot balance their need to mourn with their need to move on. He thinks back to his early days with Nancy, and how she was "like young water – energetic, joyous." While out on a run, he subconsciously heads towards the Clutter farm, and also spontaneously recalls how Mrs Kidwell claims to keep seeing Nancy riding her horse "coming this way." This is evidence of the profound psychological damage of the Clutter murders on the people of Holcomb.

The Las Vegas Arrest

Dick and Perry pick up two hitchhikers, a young boy named Bill and his ailing grandfather Johnny. They are polite, decent folk in desperate poverty, and the two men help the pair collect bottles they can exchange for coins. They earn enough to order plenty of pancakes, and they depart, wishing one another a happy new year.

On December 30th, Dewey receives word that Dick and Perry have been arrested in Las Vegas. He is overjoyed, though his nine year old son Paul is worried about him bringing these dangerous men back to Kansas, but Dewey promises that they are "not going to hurt anybody ever again."

We flashback to moments before the arrest: Perry is going into a post office to try and collect the belongings he mailed to himself while Dick waits when a police car finds them, trails them for a few blocks, and pulls up next to them. The arrest itself is not captured in the book, as we now jump forward in time again.

The Interrogations and Dick's Confession

Façade: a false or deceptive outward appearance.

Ruminate: thinking deeply about something.

On January 2nd 1960, Agents Nye and Church sit down to interview Dick, while Dewey and Duntz take Perry. Dick is "calm as could be," proudly listing the places where he passed bad cheques and boasting that he can get away with it because "people are dumb." But eventually, this **façade** crumbles when the Agents reveal they are actually questioning him about the Clutter murders, and they claim to have a "living witness" which makes Dick red with rage. He tries to maintain his innocence, so the Agents leave him to **ruminate** while they leave to watch the others interrogate Perry.

Dewey and Duntz have listened to Perry's lengthy biography, but then Duntz plays bad cop and accuses Perry of killing the Clutters. This clearly rattles him, but he claims to have never even heard the name 'Clutter' before asking for an aspirin for his leg pain. Dewey concludes the interview, "intentionally abrupt," and tells Perry that it would have been Nancy Clutter's seventeenth birthday tomorrow.

We see this technique is effective as Perry is in his cell pondering that fact. He is frustrated that he cannot talk to Dick, who is being kept in another cell, but he presumes Dick will be calm under pressure. Meanwhile, Dick is paranoid that Perry may have already confessed, and he regrets not trying to kill Floyd Wells as a loose end that has presumably led to his arrest. The interrogations continue with Nye and Church employing a method of omission – that is, deliberately not discussing the murder so that the suspect is "edgy, expectant." Finally, when Nye confronts Dick with the possibility that he will be charged with four counts of first degree murder, Dick confesses: "It was Perry. I couldn't stop him. He killed them all."

Myrtle Clare is listening to news of this confession on the radio in Hartman's Cafè, while Mrs Helm dabs her eyes, relieved that the killer has been caught. Myrtle had given an interview to the radio about how she still suspected some people in town were involved, which is an opinion several other townsfolk share, having been so wracked with suspicion and mistrust for the past few weeks.

Perry's Confession

The Agents take Perry out for a drive to try and force a confession out of him, when finally, Dewey's mention of Dick's characterisation of him as a "natural-born killer" evokes an outraged gasp, and Perry cracks. He delivers a comprehensive account of what unfolded that night – this is also the first time in the novel that we are granted this insight. When they arrived at the Clutter house, then entered through an unlocked door into Mr Clutter's office where the fail to find the supposedly money-filled safe. "Every step [they] took made a racket," as further evidence that the crime was not well planned, and they stumble into Mr Clutter's bedroom. He wakes, and the men politely bring him into his office and demand he open his safe, but Mr Clutter insists he does not have one.

Perry cuts the phone line and then hears a noise upstairs, which Dewey assumes must have been Nancy, as he had long since theorised that she had woke to hear thieves in the house and had "prudently hidden the watch, her most valuable property," in a shoe in her closet. Dick is outraged that My Clutter only has thirty dollars on hand, and demands to know if his wife has any. Mr Clutter is forced to go and wake her, but she cries that she does not, and affirms that they don't have a safe in the house. Perry claims he tries to convince Dick that the information he got from Floyd Wells was a lie, but Dick tells him to separate and tie up every member of the household until they find the safe, at which point they will "cut their throats." Dick finds Kenyon awake and forces him to get dressed when Nancy comes out of the bathrooom, "trying to smile" asking whether this is some kind of joke. Dick locks the family in the bathroom while Perry searches Nancy's room and finds a purse containing a silver dollar, which he drops and tries to retrieve from under a chair, pausing to reflect on the disgusting absurdity of a grown man "crawling on [his] belly to steal a child's silver dollar." He finds "not a dime" in Kenyon's room, but takes his radio and Mr Clutter's binoculars out to the car.

When Perry returns, they take Mr Clutter out first and Perry brings him to the basement to tie him up before doing the same to Kenyon. Mrs Clutter was "still crying" and mistrustful of Dick, but "said she felt [Perry] was a decent man" and makes him promise not to let Dick hurt her daughter. He ties Mrs Clutter up in her bedroom and finds Nancy in her bed with Dick talking to her. She tries to "act casual and friendly," making a positive impression on Perry, who listens as she describes her life and desire to go to university to study music and art. She tells him that Dick had been telling her a melodramatic life story about being an unloved orphan, while Dick continues to hunt for the safe downstairs. Perry then goes with Dick to tape up the Clutters' mouths, not wanting to leave him alone with Nancy as he threatens to rape her, and Dewey reflects that whilst Dick's story supports Perry's thusfar, he had not included this detail in his own confession. They use flashlights to navigate the house, and Mr Clutter's final words before his mouth is taped shut are him asking if his wife is okay. Perry says she is, and maintains that at that point he did not intend to "harm the man," considering him a "very nice gentleman," though after some deliberation between the two men with Dick panicking at the thought of killing Mr Clutter with a knife, Perry shoots him, and then Kenyon. Dick runs upstairs to Nancy who had started coming downstairs; she pleads with him before he shoots her in the back of the head. Mrs Clutter is the last to die, and Perry things she may have "welcomed their swift approach" after what she had heard.

Dewey feels "sorrow and profound fatigue" at having finally found the answers that he was searching for. And yet, the confessions only answer the "how and why," failing to "satisfy his sense of meaningful design. The crime was a psychological accident, virtually an impersonal act," except for the fact that they had suffered, which continues to haunt Dewey. Duntz asks Perry how much money they made from the 'robbery' to which Perry replies "between forty and fifty dollars," a pitiful sum made all the more senseless when it is viewed contextually as the cost of four innocent lives. The chapter ends with journalists descending on Garden City where Dick and Perry are brought to the courthouse, the crowd of people soon hushed to see them, "as though amazed to find them humanly shaped." Afterwards, "no one linger[s]," and snow begins to fall.

The Corner

Josie Meier

The final chapter chronicles Dick and Perry's time on death row. We meet a kind lady named Josephine Meier, wife of the undersheriff who works in the prison to cook and sew for the prisoners. She is a "practical" woman, "illuminated by a mystical serenity" such that she does not mind the company of murderers and evil men. She even worries about them going to bed on an empty stomach on their first day, so fixes them an extra meal (even though they don't appreciate this). Perry is placed in the women's prison in an effort to separate him from Dick. Josie offers to make Perry his favourite dish, and decides he is not "the worst young man [she] ever saw, though her husband, Wendle Meier, retorts that he would "cut out your heart and never bat an eye," as he experienced the crime scene for himself and considers that a better reflection of Perry's true nature.

Months pass, snow falls, Perry befriends a squirrel as well as Josie Meier, and he keeps a diary of his time in jail. He notes that he has refused to sign his own confession in which he attributes the deaths of Nancy and Mrs Clutter to Dick, as he wishes to spare Dick's "sweet" mother from the knowledge of her son's wrongdoings, though Dewey is aware that both Perry and Dick will hang regardless.

The radio, binoculars, and the two murder weapons are tracked down – the gun Nye spotted in the Hickock residence was indeed used in the crime. Perry is assigned a lawyer named Mr Arthur Flemming while Dick's is Mr Harrison Smith, and learns their case will be heard by Judge Roland H. Tate. Dick's father comes to visit him. Perry still wets the bed. He receives a letter from Don Cullivan, his friend from the army and a devout Catholic who remembers Perry fondly and offers to "help... in any way [he] can," so Perry writes a reply. Though some of these details seem mundane, this is the longest the narrative has ever stuck to Perry's perspective consistently, perhaps in Capote's effort to encourage readers to feel as though they are alongside him as he awaits his fate.

Life in Prison

We switch to Dick's windowless cell where he has other prisoners for company instead of Josie Meier, and though he managed to convince his father that he was innocent, he is spending his time fashioning a "shiv" which he thinks would "fit with lethal niceness between the shoulderblades of Undersheriff Meier" (sounds super innocent to me, dude) so he can and "bust jail," fantasising about his escape.

It is now March, and Perry is also contemplating an escape, but eventually concludes suicide is his only way out, which he dreams that he accomplishes by using the glass of a lightbulb to cut his wrists and ankles until he sees the "yellow bird" again.

The trial begins on March 22nd in front of Judge Tate, though they struggle to form a jury as it is near impossible assemble a group of people who have not heard about the crime and formed some opinion about it. The lawyers argue for a possible insanity defence, but this is countered by assistant prosecutor Logan Green who invokes the M'Naghten Rule, which **stipulates** that if an individual knows their actions were wrong, then they are sane enough to stand trial and face the consequences. Things proceed while, in the background, the Clutter home is put up for auction as life rolls on. The townsfolk bid for the Clutters' remaining farming equipment, and the property is leased to an Oklahoma ranger. Paul Helm describes this as being "like a second funeral." Even Nancy's horse is sold, and Susan gestures to wave goodbye wishing that she could adopt it like she had Nancy's cat, but instead "clasp[s her hand] over her mouth," implying she is still grieving the loss of her friend.

Stipulate: to specify or set out something.

The Trial

The court are finally able to form a jury, and everyone comes to court in their best suits, though Perry is "**sartorially** misplaced" in a shirt and jeans, looking "as lonely and inappropriate as a seagull in a wheat field." Perry and Dick submit autobiographies for the court psychiatrist, Perry's being **replete** with trauma and Dick's with his own woes of strict parents, though Dick does confess his "paedophiliac tendencies" and that he "know[s] it is wrong." Perry ends his letter expressing a desire to talk to the psychiatrist again, for he has "always felt a remarkable exhilaration being among people with a purpose and sense of dedication," which perhaps explains why he would later be so candid in interviews with Capote.

Sartorially: relating to one's clothing or fashion sense.

Replete: filled with something.

Eveanna and Beverly do not attend the trial, though Bonnie's brother Arthur does, and in spite of his earlier call for Christian forgiveness in Holcomb, he states that he "could tear them apart" when he sees Dick and Perry. The first two witnesses are Nancy Ewalt and Susan Kidwell, who found "sunshine in a bedroom, and their schoolmate, Nancy Clutter, surrounded by her own blood." The defence does not cross-examine them, presumably knowing that interrogating the traumatised teenagers about their completely accurate statements will do their clients no favours. A doctor then clarifies the method of death: "severe trauma to brain and vital cranial structures inflicted by a shotgun." This combination of both emotional and logical evidence creates a sense of an incredibly strong case. The prosecution also manages to enter into evidence the photographs taken by the Garden City Chief Investigator of Police Richard G Rohleder. Dick's father protests that the judge allowing these graphic photos be shown to the jury is proof of prejudice, shaking his head and muttering that there is "no sense having a trial."

They then call to the stand Floyd Wells, who admits that he told Dick that Mr Clutter had a safe full of money. Dick's lawyer tries to undermine Wells by asking whether his prison nickname is "Squealer" or "Snitch," though the prosecution objects to this line of questioning and they are forced to move on. Capote notes that Wells would collect the reward in exchange for him informing on Dick and Perry, though while out on parole he was arrested again in Mississippi for armed robbery and is now serving a thirty year sentence. This is a subtle indictment of the prison industrial complex in America where **recidivism** rates are high, and people like Wells are unable to escape the "**vicissitudes**" of life.

Recidivism: when a criminal reoffends.

Vicissitudes: changes of circumstances or fortune, especially unpleasant ones.

The "most damaging witness" is Alvin Dewey, who testifies to Perry's confession, including him desiring to protect Dick's parents from the knowledge of their son's cruelty, and an "anguish[ed]" Mrs Hickock breaks down in tears and has to be escorted out. She reveals that though she is full of self-reproach and cannot explain how her son could have committed such crimes, she is overwhelmed by people sending her letters of sympathy for her position, and even in Holcomb, people have not said "a mean word" to her or her husband.

Don Cullivan then takes the stand to try and save Perry's soul, and he is invited to have dinner with the Meiers and Perry in his cell. Here, Perry tells Don that he did indeed commit all four murders, quoting Willie-Jay's philosophy that all crimes were "varieties of theft" (in this case, stealing a life). Don tries to probe him to "gauge the depth of what he assumed would be Perry's **contrition**," but is dismayed to see Perry has no remorse. Perry concludes, by asking Don to help him smash a lightbulb so he can kill himself so that he may die on his own terms, but Don evidently refuses, and the trial resumes.

Contrition: feelings of remorse or penitence.

Dick's father is called to testify about his son's life and criminal history, referencing the car accident that left Dick concussed and altered his "personality and habits and actions." The next witness is Dr W Mitchell Jones who attests that Dick was able to distinguish right from wrong at the time of the crimes, but that he is "confined... by the M'Naughten Rule" which, Capote interjects is "a formula quite colour-blind to any permutations between black and white." He is legally unable to elaborate, so is dismissed, though Capote posits what Dr Jones "would have testified... had he been allowed to speak further," detailing a complex medical history of brain damage and unusual patterns of behaviour. Here, Capote implies, the law does these men a disservice by not allowing the wider story to be made apparent.

Neither of the other character witnesses – Joe James, the logger who cared for Perry during his recovery, and a Reverend who brings some of Perry's Jesus drawings from prison – fare very well for the defence either, with the prosecution dismissing many of the comments as "incompetent, irrelevant, **immaterial**." Again, Capote interpolates this with what Dr Jones "would have testified... had [he] been permitted to discourse" about Dick's "severe mental illness," and he explicates Dick's "paranoid orientation towards the world" and likely personality structure of a paranoid schizophrenic.

Immaterial: something unimportant under the circumstances.

Capote then deviates to discuss an article written by veteran forensic psychiatrist Dr Joseph Statten, "Murder Without Apparent Motive – A Study in Personality Disorganisation" which concludes that Perry was responsible for the killings, and was "logically motivated" to kill Kenyon, Nancy, and Mrs Clutter, but that the first murder of Mr Clutter occurred "under a mental eclipse, deep inside a schizophrenic darkness" where Perry sought to seek vengeance on the many metaphorical demons in his mind. Capote implicitly endorses this assessment by noting that both the professional and various amateur analysts arrive at this same conclusion.

Each side makes their final statement with prosecutor Green calling on the jury to find Dick and Perry guilty without a shadow of a doubt, guiding them through the horror the Clutters faced, each fearing for their lives and hearing one another murdered in turn, before "leav[ing] it to you [the jury] and your consciences." Though some reporters consider this heavy-handed, they mostly concern themselves with questions of good and evil, and whether the pretty much indisputable guilt of Dick and Perry would justify capital punishment.

The jury only take 40 minutes to deliberate before returning a guilty verdict, and Judge Tate solemnly echoes with "and the punishment is death" as he finds Dick and Perry guilty on all counts. They are sentenced to death as a photographer captures them laughing.

Death by Hanging

Kansas abolished the death penalty in 1907 but brought it back in 1935 to deal with some particularly heinous criminals, including the famous Bonnie and Clyde, and at the time of the Clutter murder trial, there were 190 people on death row in America, including Dick and Perry, as well as their neighbouring cellmate in the Kansas State Penitentiary, Lowell Lee Andrews who murdered his parents and sister. Capote gives us the backstory of this "brilliant son" and "adored brother" who secretly plotted to kill his doting family, though he presents this by characterising Andrews' "unsuspected personality," "stunted emotions," and "distorted mind" in order to draw attention to his mental instability. Andrews would shoot and kill his sister instantly before shooting his mother three times while she staggers in confusion, trying to speak to him, before he shoots her thrice more, and then unloading seventeen bullets into his father. This is followed by his acknowledgement that he "didn't feel anything about it," and his case would become a "legal and medical crusade" with lawyers and doctors debating the implications of a diagnosis of insanity.

Dick and Perry's initial execution dates pass as their lawyers file appeals. Perry is regularly enraged and outsmarted by Andrews correcting his grammar. Perry goes on a hunger strike and is sent to hospital. He also has persistent, haunting nightmares, and he is brought a postcard from his father than he destroys, as it resurrects feelings of "love and hate, and reminded him that he was still what he had tried not to be – alive." Two years pass, and the lawyers continue to file appeals. Dick and Perry meet George Ronald York and James Douglas Latham, two more death row prisoners who went on a killing spree together. They are another encapsulation of evil that Capote briefly examines in contrast to Dick and Perry. Dirk occupies himself by writing letters to protest his innocence that reach Everett Steerman who heads a legal aid committee, and this eventually leads to a retrial but the judge upholds the verdict and the original sentence.

Andrews is later executed, and Dick witnesses how "he danced a long time" before dying, as apparently "his heart kept beating for nineteen minutes." Perry is glad to see Andrews go though, resenting him for having had an education that was denied to Perry. Again, Capote reiterates Perry's inferiority complex and tendency to begrudge others for his own life's misfortunes. Before Andy is taken to die, Dick jokes that he'll see him soon and that Andy should "scout around" to find a "shady spot for us Down There" (in hell, even though Dick does not believe in it). In what concludes the most in-depth view we get into Dick's perspective and his own words, he remarks the people looking for "revenge" in capital punishment will never find it. He believes in hanging "just so long as [he's] not the one being hanged," but his fateful date arrives three years later.

We join Alvin Dewey to watch Dick and Perry's "long awaited" execution, announced by the ironic headline "Die on Rope for Bloody Crime," when one of our first introductions to Dick and Perry was an argument about how much rope they needed that night. Dick's is the first execution Dewey ever sees, and upon Dick's realisation that none of the Clutter family are among the witnesses, he seems "disappointed." His final words are "you people are sending me to a better world than this ever was," and he even shakes hand with the four KBI agents and says "nice to see you" with his "most charming smile... as if he were greeting guests at his own funeral." Dick is executed, and hangs for twenty minutes before being pronounced dead. The agents talk with a reporter about whether the condemned men feel anything, with one claiming he could hear him "gasping for breath."

Smith then follows, chewing gum and winking at Dewey, "jaunty and mischievous." His final words are "sombre" though, as he expresses his distaste for the death penalty and looks at his hands stained with the ink of his newfound practice of painting portraits for other inmates' children for them. He states "it would be meaningless to apologise for what I did. Even inappropriate. But I do. I apologise." Dewey closes his eyes until he hears the "thud-snap that announces a rope-broken neck," finding himself more affected by Perry's death than Dick's, for Dick seemed to him ultimately just a "small-time chiseller who got out of his depth, empty and worthless." By contrast, Perry is in Dewey's estimation "a true murderer" and yet had "the aura of an exiled animal, a creature walking wounded," and Dewey is haunted by his "childish feet... dangling."

Dewey and Susan

Dewey notes that he did not feel a sense of climactic finality upon Dick and Perry's execution, and instead recalls an incident from the previous year where he had a chance encounter with Susan Kidwell while they are each visiting the Clutter graves. Susan is now a college junior studying art, and reflects on the dreams she once shared with Nancy Clutter. She informs Dewey that Bobby has since married another wonderful girl, though she soon has to run off, and Dewey watches her go thinking that she is the kind of "young woman... Nancy might have been." The novel ends with him heading home, "leaving behind him the big sky, the whisper of wind voices in the wind-bent wheat" – a solemn and plaintive embodiment of Dewey leaving the case and the tragedy in the past, just as others in Holcomb have done in order to carry on with their lives.

Section 4

Character Analysis

There are *a lot* of characters in this text, no doubt a result of Capote's robust research and interviews. Here, I have listed what I consider the major characters, as well as four main categories of minor characters. Obviously these major ones should be your primary concern, and this is where you should draw most of your evidence from, but the veritable array of side characters are also very important, so try to familiarise yourself with most of them to use as supplementary examples in your essays!

Mr Herb Clutter

Mr Clutter is a "very nice gentleman" – even his murderers agree! He is a benevolent presence in Holcomb and a devoted family man who runs the farm and pays his employees generously. He also dedicates himself to his community through the "4-H Club" which embodies the four values Herb holds dear: "Head, Heart, Hands, Health." He loves his wife and worries greatly for her mental health, he is proud of his eldest daughters and their choice of husband/fiancé respectively, he is especially close with Nancy who is in every way the golden child (though her relationship with Bobby causes some tension), and he holds affection for his young and only son Kenyon who he knows is unlikely to grow up to manage the farm one day but will hopefully find his way in life. Though Mr Clutter is not a two-dimensionally flawless man, he is undeniably a good man, and Capote repeatedly affirms this from the perspective of multiple characters.

However, we only get to know Mr Clutter very briefly, and one could argue that there is a degree of **whitewashing** that occurs after someone's death; it is almost suspicious that everyone in town thinks fondly of Herb and cannot think of anyone who could possibly have a grudge against him. This characterisation also compounds the senselessness and confusion in the wake of the murders, for the conventional explanations of a crime like domestic violence or a rival lover are quickly dismissed by both town gossip and law enforcement.

Whitewash: to make something bad seem more acceptable by hiding the truth.

There is an acknowledgement that his relationship with his wife is troubled, as her poor health hinders her from fulfilling the conventional role of a farmer's wife or taking part in and hosting family gatherings. They even sleep in separate rooms because of how **disparate** their lives are – Herb is awake at 6:30 and ready to work, whereas Bonnie struggles to get out of bed most days. Furthermore, as a Methodist he harbours some prejudicial views towards Bobby Rupp for being a Catholic, which leads to conflict between him and Nancy, though neither of these two things are implied to be insurmountable. Rather, they are mundane family problems that are now frozen in time, with no one left alive to resolve them. Ultimately, Capote building up Mr Clutter as a family man and valuable presence in the community makes the sudden loss of him all the more stark.

Disparate: completely different and incomparable.

Mrs Bonnie Clutter

Although all of the Clutter deaths are incredibly tragic, there is something especially poignant about the death of Bonnie Clutter, a woman struggling to live with many regrets, and afflicted by terrible postnatal depression that has accumulated into a chronic **despondency** and **convalescence**. She once had dreams of pursing a career in nursing (a path that her second eldest daughter Beverly would go on to fulfil, perhaps one of the few hopeful elements of the novel!) and she bitterly laments that she did not see this through "just to prove... that [she] once succeeded at something." This revelation also implies she does not consider her flourishing family a 'success' she has achieved, for she fears they "don't need [her]." These feelings of inadequacy create a **self-fulfilling prophecy** whereby Bonnie retreats from her own life, with Nancy (perhaps unconsciously) filling the void by learning to prepare family meals and compensate for her mother's absence.

Despondency: low spirits or dejection from a loss of hope.

Convalescence: time spent recuperating from an illness or medical treatment.

Self-fulfilling prophecy: when a prediction comes true because one's awareness leads to one fulfilling it.

To her credit though, Bonnie is a good judge of character: in the short time she is exposed to the cruelty of Dick and Perry, she deduces that Dick is the more outwardly brutal and sadistic, and that he may harbour vicious intentions towards Nancy, whereas she views Perry as a more reliable man, making him promise not to let Dick harm her daughter. Though she may be wrong to consider Perry trustworthy, he does fulfil his promise to her, and it is likely that Bonnie's insights and pleas were what prevented Nancy from enduring more pain and trauma before her death.

After one of many stays at a psychiatric facility, Bonnie learns that her psychological anguish may be the result of a pinched nerve in her spine, but in yet another tragedy, we will never know if that was truly the case. In some sense, Bonnie's sense of unfulfilment persists after her death as Capote explores the consequences of the murders, and the senselessness behind them.

Nancy Clutter

Nancy is a sixteen year old golden girl whose overachieving tendencies are evident in the dozens of commitments she keeps on the day of her death. She is an accomplished musician, student, horse rider, chef, and community leader who also takes time to tutor other young girls in her various talents. In some sense, she fulfils the role of the household matriarch, despite only being a teenager, as her mother is often unable to do so. That she does this with a "radiant jauntiness" furthers this image of her as a perfect daughter, as her disposition makes it hard for anyone to resent or be jealous of her. She even engages with Perry on the night of the murder and attempts to talk to him, demonstrating her bravery and maturity.

Like her father, Nancy is just fundamentally *good* and hence her unrealised potential is all the more tragic. As with all of the Clutter deaths, Nancy's is a life left unfulfilled – would she have gone on to defy her father and pursue a relationship with Bobby? Would she have one day left Holcomb and accomplished something great? Her death means these are just some of the many questions in the text we will never know the answer to.

Kenyon Clutter

Kenyon is a somewhat sensitive boy who is still in the process of forging and coming to terms with his identity and physicality when he is tragically killed at the age of fourteen. Whilst he is also a straight-A student, he is more flawed than Nancy, needing to wear glasses and being a "lanky" boy ill-adjusted to his six foot height, and though he partakes in team sports he only has one real friend who soon drifts away in favour of a girlfriend. But Kenyon is relatively content in his own company, and has solitary hobbies like dismantling machinery or reading books, and Mr Clutter thinks he could one day be an engineer or a scientist.

In many ways, Nancy takes after her father in being an impeccably and universally admired member of Holcomb, whilst Kenyon is more like his mother in feeling somewhat out of place. Our thoughts and feelings about his relationships and his future are cut short, however, as he is killed alongside his family.

Richard Eugene 'Dick' Hickock

Dick is in many ways the more evil of the two killers. A head injury early in life led to him adopting more psychopathic tendencies, though his upbringing wasn't as turbulent as Perry's. He has an ex-wife whom he claims to love, but she left him when he cheated on her and got another woman pregnant, whom he subsequently married then abandoned. Despite is relatively high IQ, he becomes a creature of impulse, and has little capacity to distinguish right from wrong. This is most evident in the crimes he commits – not only the murder of the Clutters, but his molestation of young girls. Though he is "sincerely ashamed" of this, he is unable to suppress these **carnal** desires, which is further proof of his diminished psychological capacity. He is apparently only prevented from raping Nancy Clutter by Perry, who detests the idea.

Carnal: relating to sexual or lustful activities.

These impulse-control tendencies align with another common psychopathic trait of over-confidence. He regularly dismisses Perry's concerns about the possibility of getting caught, though there are many flags throughout the novel that Dick is not the criminal mastermind he thinks he is. Rather, Dick is a conscience-less killer, and in many ways a distillation of the most selfish, evil parts of humanity. His relationship with Perry is complicated the men only share "surface level" similarities with Perry being more artistic and Dick being the "literal minded" one, and at times their personalities clash. Dick had been intrigued by Perry's claim to have killed a man with a bicycle chain, and once considered Perry "a natural killer – absolutely sane, but conscienceless and capable of dealing, with or without motive, the coldest-blooded deathblows," though this is not remotely true.

Perry would claim in a confession that Dick killed Mrs and Nancy Clutter himself, but he refused to sign his name to verify this, and would instead take the blame for all four deaths, which was the story Dick insisted on (further evidence of his self-interest).

Readers are typically less inclined to empathise with Dick due to his lack of self-reflection. Where Perry is more self-aware and self-critical, Dick's anarchy and recklessness makes him seem rather impulsive and unlikable.

He is the first of the two to be executed, though more time is devoted to Perry's hanging, for Dewey considers Dick a "small-time chiseller who got out of his depth, empty and worthless."

Perry Edward Smith

Perry is a complex and damaged man. Though Capote delves into his disadvantaged upbringing and history of abuse and pain to unearth elements of Perry's intelligence, sensitivity, and talent, he nevertheless refrains from glorifying Perry as an antihero, as he also makes it clear Perry repeatedly and deliberately chooses to go down a self-destructive path. Possibly because of Capote's affinity for Perry which developed over the course of him interviewing Perry for his novel, Capote emphasises Perry's artistic side, but he also has Dewey note that Perry seems like "the true murderer" of the story.

It is likely Perry was a paranoid schizophrenic with this condition either caused or exacerbated by his traumatic childhood. His mother is an alcoholic who dies choking on her own vomit having lived a miserable life of domestic abuse, and his father soon abandons him – a "hated, hating half-breed child" (Perry was half-**Cherokee**) – in the care of nuns whose abuse leaves him with a life-long hatred for them (and perhaps even religion as a whole). Two of his sisters commit suicide, and he is unable to form close relationships with anyone else in his family. Capote also includes various details that some critics have argued humanise Perry too much, making him excessively sympathetic, such as the fact that he wets the bed and cries himself to sleep like a child. However, we could also argue that these add to the tragedy Capote attempts to explore – although Perry was criminally responsible for his actions that night on the Clutter farm, he had very little control over the other events in his life that shaped him, making him a compelling character if not a wholly sympathetic one.

Cherokee: a group of Native American people in the south-eastern US.

There are many contradictory elements to Perry's character. He did not receive a formal education, but he has an inexplicably sophisticated vocabulary. He appears to be the more sensible, thoughtful, and sympathetic of the two killers, but he is also at times undeniably brutal. And in one of my favourite lines of the text, Capote describes how "the quietness of his tone italicised the malice of his reply," which hints at an unfathomably dark and sinister side to Perry.

He detests any talk of sex (particularly from Dick) but could be said to perhaps harbour some homosexual tendencies towards Dick or other male figures he pursues in his life, such as Willie-Jay, though it is equally possible he is asexual with a complete aversion to physical intimacy, and this may just be a desperate search for any kind of attachment, given this was denied to him in childhood. It is implied that he has sex with Cookie, but he describes this as "strange" and regards their potential love or marriage with a degree of detachment such that she is now just "a girl [he] almost married."

Perry briefly joins the army but then abandons this to become a vagabond before he is severely injured in a motorbike accident. His constant pain leads to him developing an addiction to aspirin. Out of pity for Dick's mother, Perry claims responsibility for all four murders, and he dies uttering the plangent quote "Maybe I had something to contribute, something –" before apologising.

The letter Willie-Jay leaves Perry upon his release from prison is a very useful passage in helping us understand Perry's character, as he **candidly** explicates Perry's fundamental character flaws and the danger he is in if these go unchecked. The contradictory nature of Perry is perhaps best summarised by one of the novel's most famous quotes: "I thought [Mr Clutter] was a very nice gentleman. I thought so right up to the moment I cut his throat." That Perry can make judgements about people's character and yet commit such heinous acts makes it hard for us, as well as for the law enforcement figures and officers of the court, to determine his criminal capacity and mental sanity.

Candidly: in a frank or straightforward manner.

Agent Alvin Dewey

Dewey is effectively the hero of the story. Himself a Kansas family man who knew the Clutters, the case is personal for him and becomes an all-consuming "fixation." Capote celebrates his patient and effective investigation, as Dewey's methodical policework eventually leads to the capture of the two guilty parties. Though he does not seem overly emotional, his investment in the case is a testament to how affected he is by it, which takes a toll on his own family life.

Dewey's wife Marie is also present in some scenes; herself the daughter of an FBI agent, she is a knowledgeable and sympathetic character mostly designed to comfort Dewey during the confronting and **protracted** investigation.

Protracted: long or overly extended.

For the most part, Dewey's motivations align with ours, as readers, though at times we are a few steps ahead as we are aware of who the killers are. But once they are captured, we and Dewey alike are desperate to uncover the motivation for the crime.

In the end, Dewey is our witness to the executions of Dick and Perry, and while he barely remarks on the former, the death of Perry troubles him somewhat, as Perry had "the aura of an exiled animal, a creature walking wounded."

Minor characters: Clutter family and friends

Eveanna Jarchow and Beverly English (née Clutter)

Eveanna and Beverly are the two eldest Holcomb children who have already moved out of home and thus are not murdered along with the rest of their family. Eveanna is already married and has a son who is less than a year old when the crime occurs, while Beverly is studying nursing and engaged to be married to a man named Vere English. Both of their husbands are white collar professionals, and though this means they are not candidates to one day take over the Clutter farm, Mr Clutter still approves greatly of these relationships, noting that the men are well positioned to take care of his daughters (this judgement is highly steeped in patriarchal norms, but it nevertheless presented in a positive light in the text).

Susan and Wilma Kidwell

Susan Kidwell is Nancy's best friend, and conveys her concern for her in relation to Nancy's ongoing conflict with her father over her relationship with Bobby. The Kidwells moved to Holcomb when Susan was eight, a "melancholy, imaginative child, willowy and wan and sensitive" but left fatherless as Mr Kidwell abandoned his wife and child. The Clutters practically "adopted" her and came to treat Susan as a member of their own family, and though she transfers to a different school, she remains very close with Nancy. This serves to amplify the tragic loss of the Clutters, as Susan must face the acute loss of her dearest friend as well as a surrogate family that showed her so much kindness. Susan gives a police statement and later testifies in court.

Her mother, Wilma Kidwell, teaches music at Holcomb School and lives with her daughter at the Teacherage. It is implied she also wrestles with grief in the wake of the murders as she hallucinates Nancy riding her horse nearby.

Bobby Rupp

Bobby Rupp is Nancy Clutter's boyfriend, and by all accounts the two are very much in love. Mr Clutter quietly disapproves of their relationship as Bobby's family is Catholic whereas the Clutters are Methodists, but he permits Nancy to continue seeing him on the condition that it does not become more serious. The fact that Nancy was increasingly invested in this relationship is a source of some tension between her and her father until their deaths, and Bobby is left utterly shocked by the sudden and violent death of his girlfriend. He also wrestles with a sense of survivor's guilt and regret, as he had wanted to take Nancy out to the movies on Saturday night but Mr Clutter refused, so they had made plans for Sunday instead.

In the aftermath of the murders, he is briefly considered a suspect but passes a lie detector test and is cleared. Though he was once close with Nancy's friends, particularly Susan, he gradually distances himself from them, unable to engage with memories of her.

Nancy and Clarence Ewalt

Nancy Ewalt is a close friend of Nancy Clutter, and together with Susan Kidwell is part of the first party to discover their friend's dead body, having gone to the Clutters Sunday morning before church. She is greatly traumatised by these events, and her father Mr Ewalt brings her back home so he and Larry Hendricks can go investigate. Nancy will later testify alongside Susan at the trial, reliving the dreadful memory of seeing her friend's body and the shotgun blast of blood on the walls of her room.

Jolene Katz

Jolene is the young girl who visits the Clutter house the day before they die as her mother requests Nancy show Jolene how to bake a cherry pie. After doing so, Jolene waits for her mother to pick her up and is kept company by Mrs Clutter, though she is slightly perturbed by the older woman's fragile mental state and self-deprecating references to how her family "don't need [her]" as their mother.

Alfred Stoecklein

Alfred is the only Clutter employee who lives on the farm, residing with his wife and three children about 100 metres away from the Clutter home. He takes the morning off on the day the Clutters are killed so that he and his wife can take their sick baby to the hospital. Herb granting him this leave and "expressing sympathy" contributes to our sense of him as a generous and compassionate man. On the night of the murders, the couple are nursing the baby in their home but do not hear the gunshots. Alfred becomes one of many characters that the people of Holcomb suspect, and this coupled with their proximity to the tragedy is enough to drive them out of their property and to another house in town.

Mr Paul and Mrs Mabel Helm

Mrs Helm is the shy Clutter housekeeper who does her best to change Mrs Clutter's bedsheets on the rare occasions when she is not confined to her bed by her chronic depression. After the murders, she is the one who notices Kenyon's radio is missing, which is one of the only things Dick and Perry stole in their aborted attempt at robbery. She later goes to work at Hartman's Cafè where she withholds her knowledge of the crime scene from prying townsfolk.

Mr Helm is one of the characters who is 'The Last to See Them Alive' in the eponymous first chapter, and he notes that there was "nothing out of the ordinary" about that day or their interactions. When the Clutter farm is auctioned off and he moves away, he remarks that it feels like "a second funeral."

Minor characters: Dick and Perry's associates

Mr Walter and Mrs Hickock

Dick's parents are farmers who welcome him home the day after the murder for Sunday dinner, completely unaware of the crime their son has committed. Unlike Perry, they provided a stable family home for Dick, but his head injury damaged his psyche in ways they could not fathom. Though Mrs Hickock is initially averse to Perry, he considers her such a sweet woman that he takes responsibility for all four murders so that she would not have to live with the knowledge that her son was such a vicious killer. Mr Hickock maintains some belief in his son's innocence, protesting that the judge is biased during the trial. Meanwhile, Mrs Hickock just tries to catch her son's eye and "simulat[e] a smile which, though flimsily constructed, affirmed her loyalty." Ultimately, they are unconditionally loving parents, who are in "anguish" over the circumstances their son is in, and Mrs Hickock in particular is shocked to discover how compassionate people are to their situation, even in Holcomb, where no one has said "a mean word" to them. When she learns of Perry's efforts to conceal Dick's violent and predatory nature from her, she reflects that where once she hated Perry, now she just pities him as a "dying" man.

John 'Tex' Smith and Julia 'Flo' Buckskin

Perry's parents are far less stable than Dick's. Tex Smith was a "homely-handsome Irish cowboy" while Flo was a Native American girl who worked as a "professional rodio performer" before they met, married, and had four children, three of whom would meet tragic ends. Despite a few happy years when the rodeo performing couple live with their four children, a messy divorce leaves Flo an embittered alcoholic, and she dies choking on her own vomit having lived her final years in a drunken **stupor**, prostituting herself to get by.

Stupor: a state of near-unconsciousness or insensibility.

Tex eventually gains custody of Perry (though abandons his other children to the foster care system, perhaps due to the patriarchal society's preference for the first born son) and teaches him to fish and hunt. He later submits a "biography" of Perry's traumatic life to the court in order to grant him parole for his petty theft charges. However, Perry's attempts to live with him in Alaska afterwards end with them literally trying to kill each other – Tex is only unsuccessful because the gun he fires at his son is not loaded. This fractured relationship is never mended, and likely the cause of Perry's various psychological hang-ups and attachment issues.

Barbara Johnson

Barbara Johnson is the one child of Tex and Flo that does not seem to have been afflicted by crippling mental illnesses. She "entered ordinary life, married" and had "begun raising a family," while all of her siblings die by either suicide or execution. We hear her perspective first in a letter she writes to Perry while he is in prison in which she implores him to take responsibility for his own actions, though he uses an analysis written by Willie-Jay to counter this in his mind.

As a result of Willie-Jay's letter, Perry is able to dismiss Barbara as a hypocrite who only finds it easy to "ignore the rain" because she "ha[s] a raincoat" (i.e. she has escaped a life of hardship and trauma). This is something of a turning point in our estimation of Perry though, as we start to see signs of a man deep in denial about his own inadequacies, and determined to deflect responsibility onto his father, his abusive upbringing at the hands of "Black Widow" nuns, or society as a whole. Agent Nye also goes to meet with Barbara as part of his investigation, and learns Perry's backstory from her, after which she "bolt[s]" her door closed in an attempt to protect herself from her family history.

Fern 'Joy' Smith

Fern is the sibling whom Perry is most fond of, and he remembers her as "such a sweet person... artistic... a terrific dancer," and someone who could have "got somewhere" in life if she were luckier. Though Perry tried to convince himself that she fell, she killed herself at nineteen by jumping out of a fifteen storey hotel window – another senseless tragedy. That she changes her name to 'Joy' at fourteen and spends "the rest of her short life tr[ying] to justify the replacement" is bitterly ironic given her suicide and likely mental struggles.

Jimmy Smith

Jimmy is Perry's only brother, a Navy officer who kills himself after having shot his wife the day prior, suspicious of her supposed infidelity, though it is implied he was paranoid. His story is one of several Smith tragedies, and supports the notion of a family history of mental illness.

Floyd Wells

Floyd is the person who while in prison erroneously informs Dick that Mr Clutter has $10,000 in a safe inside his property, and is hence the unwitting catalyst for the murders. As a former employee of Mr Clutter, he is able to give Dick a detailed description of the house's layout, though he only persists with the lie believing that Dick would never attempt to carry out a robbery. He redeems himself by confessing what he told Dick, which is what leads to Dick and Perry's capture, and testifying against them in their trial. Although he earns a reward and parole for having ensured their conviction, he is back in prison in no time, serving as an example of the cyclical recidivism in the American criminal justice system.

Willie-Jay

Willie-Jay is a fellow inmate of Perry's at the Kansas State Penitentiary, and despite their brief time together, he leaves a lasting impression. As the chaplain's clerk, Willie-Jay is a man of God who attempts to instil an appreciation for religion and morals in Perry, though he struggles due to Perry's stubborn nature. He leaves Perry a scathing letter that astutely identifies his most fundamental fears and flaws, ultimately in an attempt to warn Perry that he cannot continue to resent others for their happiness. He also identifies something dangerous that lurks in Perry's core: an "explosive emotional" centre that is "out of all proportion to the occasion." We then see the culmination of this in Perry's behaviour at the Clutter home, suggesting Willie-Jay was incredibly perceptive in his assessment of Perry.

However, Perry sees his greatest critic as perhaps his greatest friend, and will later try to fill the void left behind in Willie-Jay's absence with Dick who is in many ways **antithetical**. Perry believes Willie-Jay to be the only one who truly sees his "worth" and his "potentialities," finding solace in his support. Willie-Jay moves east after he is released from prison for petty theft, and Perry is disappointed to later learn he has left Kansas despite their tumultuous friendship. His message continues to haunt Perry, though it is clear Perry does not learn from this in time.

Antithetical: contrasting, or mutually incompatible.

Joe James

Joe is an Indian logger who cares for Perry after his motorcycle accident, and testifies at his trial about Perry being a "likeable kid," and later, a "likeable fellow." Unsurprisingly, this is not sufficient in saving Perry from death row.

Lowell Lee Andrews

Andrews is on death row at the same time as Perry and Dick, having murdered his own parents and sister. He is a diagnosed schizophrenic but due to Kansas' M'Naghten Rule, this is not enough to save him from his execution, which occurs three years before the hanging of Perry and Dick. He is a thorn in Perry's side during their imprisonment together, as he is just as if not more intelligent than Perry, but demonstrates this by correcting his grammar to annoy him. Andrews is "without malice, but Perry could have boiled him in oil," which is evidence of his untempered rage and delusions, and perhaps also proof that Perry is too mentally unwell to have learned any moral lessons by his imprisonment.

Cookie

Cookie is a nurse who cares for Perry after his accident, and she becomes the girl Perry "almost marrie[s]." This is not a conventional relationship, as it begins with her having "pitied him" and "babied him" before "sexual episodes of a strange and stealthy nature had occurred," likely indicative of Perry's attachment disorder (or as some critics have postulated, his homosexuality or asexuality) before he leaves her with a poem he pretends to have written.

Bill and Johnny

Bill is a young, incredibly impoverished boy who is living on the streets with his old, sick grandfather Johnny. The pair meet Dick and Perry while they are on the run, and together they hunt for enough bottles to exchange for money to buy food. Billy has a sunny optimism despite his circumstances, and is an example of a struggling character making the best of a terrible situation.

Don Cullivan

Don meets Perry while they are serving in the military, but like Willie-Jay, he finds religion and attempts to bring Perry to God, though is likewise unsuccessful. He testifies in Perry's defence at the trial and attempts to make a case for Christian forgiveness.

Minor characters: people of Holcomb

Larry Hendricks

Hendricks is Holcomb's English teacher and school bus driver who goes with Mr Ewalt and the sheriff to the Clutter home after the murders. His penchant for writing stories and him thinking to himself that he must remember every detail of the scene in case he needs to testify in court makes for an incredibly evocative account as the men discover all four dead bodies, and try in vain to piece together what could have occurred. Hendricks is our lens into the horrors of the crime scene, and his confusion mirrors our own as readers as we are exposed to the haunting details that he observes.

Mrs Hideo Ashida

Mrs Ashida and her family were welcomed into Holcomb two years previously and have a particularly close relationship with the Clutters. This is all largely **symbiotic**, as the community provide fresh produce and farming assistance to the Ashidas while they establish themselves, and in turn Mrs Ashida nourishes the community with her delicious soups! She is also a member of the 4-H Club, and Mr Clutter nominates her for an award for her contributions shortly before he is killed. Though she and her husband mention they are contemplating leaving for Nebraska before the murders, the deaths of the Clutters upset her greatly and she feels she has no choice but to leave town.

Symbiotic: a mutually beneficial relationship.

Mrs Bess Hartman

Mrs Bess Hartman is the owner of Harman's Cafè where citizens of Holcomb meet to discuss the events that unfold in town. She is an "unfoolish lady" with "authoritative green eyes" and the cousin of Mrs Myrtle Clare. She relays the gossip she overhears from her patrons, as well as her own theories about how and why the murders of the Clutters took place.

Mrs Sadie 'Mother' Truitt and Mrs Myrtle Clare

Sadie 'Mother' Truitt is the old postmistress of Holcomb, and is described as a "**gaunt**" 75 year old woman wearing a "babushka bandannas" and a "rawhide jacket and denims and cowboy boots." Hence, not only is she conspicuously Southern, her appearance also mirrors the "falling-apart post office" in which she works – it is as though both the buildings and the people of Holcomb are gaunt and run-down. (She's also my favourite character because she hangs out in the ramshackle post office with her coffee and a good book, contently watching the world go by!)

Gaunt: lean, haggard, or emaciated, especially because of suffering, hunger, or age.

She is the oldest resident who was born in Holcomb, and it is implied she has been there her whole life, just as her daughter Myrtle will after her, having followed in her mother's footsteps to take on the duties of delivering mail. Myrtle takes after her mother in many ways, though with the addition of a "rooster-crow" voice and more opinionated demeanour.

The two women observe the ambulances drive to the Holcomb residence on Sunday morning, and Mother Truitt's horrified reaction and subsequent confrontation of her own mortality is used as an analogy for the reaction of Holcomb as a whole.

Myrtle is often the representation for the town's gossip and theorising, and she even maintains after Dick and Perry's arrest that there *must* be some deeper conspiracy involving people in town. She is the embodiment of the desperate search for meaning amidst madness.

Mr and Mrs Bob Johnson

Bob Johnson is the man who meets with Herb Clutter the Saturday before he is killed to sell him a new life insurance policy. He is stunned by the fact that he met with a man to discuss life insurance just hours before he was murdered, resulting in a double indemnity (i.e. a payout of twice what the insurance was worth) for his remaining children, and though he legally does not have to do so, he decides it is morally right to make good on this agreement.

Jonathan Daniel Adrian

Adrian is a man of "no fixed address" who briefly shelters in the Clutter home while drifting to New Mexico, completely unaware of the tragedy. He is seen by Paul Helm who calls the sheriff, and Adrian shows them how he crawled through a pipe that led into the basement. He is then arrested when the investigators find a shotgun and a hunting knife in his car, though is later ruled out as a suspect.

Minor characters: forces of justice

Sheriff Robinson

The Holcomb sheriff is one of the first men on scene at the Clutter home, and is called out again when Paul Helm spots Adrian having broken into the Clutter home.

Josephine Meier

Josephine Meier is married to Garden City's Undersheriff Wendel Meier. She is a remarkably compassionate woman who fulfils the rather thankless job of serving as a cook and seamstress at the county jail. She meets Perry while he is imprisoned there and takes pity on him, preparing a fancy meal for him and Don Cullivan when he visits. Her tendency to see the best in people is dismissed by her husband, who says her opinion of Perry would be far less generous if she had seen the bodies of the Clutters. Nevertheless, she holds Perry's hand when the guilty verdict is delivered and he is sentenced to death.

Special Agents Harold Nye, Roy Church, and Clarence Duntz

Nye is the youngest member of the KBI investigation team, but is responsible for discovering most of the incriminating evidence. He is also tasked with interviewing the remaining members of the Clutter family, and learns that "of all the people in all the world, the Clutters were the least likely to be murdered." He and Church are responsible for interrogating Dick upon his capture, while Dewey and Duntz interrogate Perry. They do not play a major role in the book, which is something Capote was criticised for; many claimed he aggrandised the role of Alvin Dewey for the sake of having a more cohesive, single hero, when in reality it is thought that these other men were just as important to the investigation.

Arthur Fleming

Fleming is Perry's lawyer in the murder trial. He is an "old... classic country lawyer more happy at home with land deeds than ill deeds," but does his best to advocate for Perry.

Harrison Smith

Smith is Dick's lawyer in the murder trial and accepts the task with "resigned grace" knowing that someone must fulfil this unpalatable role. He is a "mild and lenient man" though adopts an "aggressive" manner when questioning Floyd Wells on the stand.

Judge Roland Tate

Tate is the judge in Dick and Perry's murder trial. One of the jury members later tells Capote that Tate is a "lawbook lawyer" who "never experiments [and] foes strictly by the text," and that if they were on trial, Tate is either the best judge to have if you are innocent or the worst one if you are guilty.

Duane West and Logan Green

West is the county attorney tasked with prosecuting the case against Dick and Perry. He is an ambitious 28 year old who appears 40 or 50, and pursues the death penalty as he argues Dick and Perry deserve worse than Kansas' second most severe sentence of "life imprisonment" which typically only amounts to less than fifteen years.

Green is the assistant prosecuting attorney and is the one to explain they can use the M'Naghten Rule to counter a defence of insanity. He becomes a "star" of the trial and delivers the closing remarks, calling on the jury to find Dick and Perry guilty without "a single doubt."

Section 5

Key Themes Analysis

Justice and the morality of the death penalty

Regardless of your personal views on capital punishment, this book raises some probing questions. Can a punishment ever fit a crime? Who are we really trying to help by killing killers? And what are the ethics of prosecuting the criminally insane? For the most part, Capote seems to align himself with the views Perry expresses shortly before he dies – that "it's a helluva thing to take a life in this manner."

The novel also critiques the criminal justice system. Whilst we can celebrate the KBI team and their investigation, the actions of the legal team are more morally ambiguous. The prosecutors, West and Green, use powerful rhetoric and seemingly **unassailable** logic in constructing the case against Dick and Perry, and though they are obviously guilty, there are some voices in the text that criticise how strongly they pursue this, making a guilty verdict and hence death penalty sentence seemingly inevitable. Whether Capote endorses these voices is another matter, but he *does* include them in the text, which is a meaningful authorial choice.

Unassailable: unable to be attacked, questioned, or defeated.

We are also not particularly inclined to celebrate other characters being on death row or in jail. Capote's reference to how Floyd Wells will be incarcerated once again after breaking his parole, this time serving thirty years in Mississippi, prompts us to reflect on the **purpose of imprisonment:**

- Does it **deter** the criminal from offending again?
- Does it deter others from committing similar acts?
- Does it keep the wider community safer?
- Does it provide some sense of justice to the victims?

Deter: to dissuade someone from doing something.

This question of a 'sense of justice' is another key concept in *In Cold Blood.* Dewey, among other characters, often remarks that many things about the Clutter case don't feel right, from their bodies on the day of the murders to the sensation Dewey feels as he watches Dick and Perry hang. While we are listening to Perry confess, Dewey's thoughts interrupt to ponder the "prolonged terror" the Clutters endured, and how they waited "without any premonition of their destiny" before being killed one by one. This clearly contrasts with the experiences of death row inmates, who know "their date" with the hangman will "arrive," and Dick even jokes with other inmates about saving a place for one another in hell.

While on death row, Perry has violent thoughts towards his neighbouring inmate Lowell Lee Andrews – perhaps this suggests he is incapable of seeing the error of his ways, and that he should therefore be executed as an irredeemable villain. Or perhaps this is proof that Perry lacks the mental capacity to understand or benefit from punishment and that he hence cannot ever adequately be punished, so what point does the death penalty serve?

Mental illness and insanity

This theme is very closely linked to questions of justice and punishment. Both Perry and Dick are thought to be paranoid schizophrenics, Perry potentially inheriting a family history of mental illness that is exacerbated by an abusive childhood, whilst Dick's condition is only set in motion later in life with a concussion leading to violent tendencies and impulse control problems. In the text and in real life, they were found guilty and medically insane, but *legally sane* because of the M'Naghten Rule, as they were deemed to have understood the wrongness of their criminal acts. Capote criticises this for its "colour-blind[ness]" and clearly intimates his belief that this was unfair on Dick and Perry, and many other criminals alike. He offers detailed reports from the psychiatrists who examined them, lamenting that their contents are what the doctors "would have testified" to in court, had they been permitted. Plainly, Capote gives us this information because he believes it should have been given to the jury too.

The American dream

The archetypal American Dream, in literature and in history, was the idea of 'equality of opportunity' – in theory, anyone could achieve the 'dream' of a nuclear family in a white-picket-fenced home. But what *In Cold Blood* represents is a kind of **American nightmare,** as this household of good Christian citizens, led by the "very nice gentleman" Herb Clutter, are brutally killed on an otherwise ordinary day, for seemingly no reason. If the American Dream is meant to inspire hope in its population by suggesting that everyone can reach their goals, the American nightmare is a stark reminder of just how fragile all this is. The American Dream puts all of the onus onto individuals – you can accomplish anything if only you work hard enough, but what this story shows us is that sometimes apparently random acts can unjustly destroy this dream, and there are some forces in life outside of our control.

Dick and Perry, therefore, represent these forces and they embrace an **anarchic** desire to do whatever they please, though they themselves are subject to the disappointment of unfulfilled dreams. We see them try to map out plans to travel to the **utopia** of Mexico City, but they are soon underwhelmed, broke, and forced to hitchhike back where they came from. This geographical aimlessness mirrors their lack of psychological drive and direction, as they are unable to build constructive lives for themselves, but also refuse to take responsibility for their actions.

Anarchic: with no controlling rules or principles to provide order.

Utopia: a seemingly perfect world.

Tragedy amidst normality

Many pages of *In Cold Blood* are dedicated to establishing the normality and familiarity of the Clutters and Holcomb. You may not be familiar with any 1950s Kansas farming families yourself, but you are immediately drawn in to the world of cheerful patriarch Herb, his ailing wife, his perfect daughter, and his curious son. That they are a typical **nuclear family** furthers the perception of them as a microcosmic American household, in a quiet and peaceful town whose name most people didn't even know.

Nuclear family: the typical social structure of a husband, wife, and their children.

All of this establishment is designed to make the loss of the Clutters in the community so much more palpable. Had the story began at Chapter 2, we would not have the same affinity for this family, nor the same horror at the manner of their murder.

Capote is a proficient writer, following the golden rule of 'show, don't tell' in the tragedy's aftermath. He never says "everybody in Holcomb was really sad and scared" but this is the sense we get from the **vignettes** of townsfolk in Hartman's Cafè. In both the lead up to the crime and its aftermath, Capote **lauds** the Clutters and their memory, amplifying the sense of devastation felt in their absence.

Vignette: a brief, evocative description or episode.

Laud: to praise highly.

Senselessness

This novel is not a 'whodunnit.' We know, very early on in the text, that it was Dick and Perry who committed these crimes. And for many in Capote's **contemporary** audience, the Clutters and their killers may well have been household names. Instead, this is a text that only briefly concerns itself with the *how*, and then becomes fixated on the *why*.

Contemporary: 'of the same time' – in this case, we are talking about readers in the 1960s when the book was published.

But when we find out the answer, and that the Clutters were killed for "between forty and fifty dollars" in a misguided attempted robbery based on false information, this does not feel like a satisfying resolution. It was a senseless tragedy that did not need to happen, but was set in motion by unfortunate circumstances, a cocktail of nature and nurture that warped two men into dangerously violent criminals, and the inability of these two mentally ill men to take responsibility for their own actions. Subsequently, they are apprehended, receive a fair trial, and are found guilty before being executed. But what was the point of this? Dick and Perry don't seem to have learned anything, and those in attendance do not experience a climactic relief. Instead, as Capote suggests with the novel's ending, life goes on, tragedies recede, and sometimes there is no meaning to be found in madness.

Masculinity

Almost all of the male major characters in the text seek to conform to masculine stereotypes in some way. Mr Clutter is the **prototypical** "man's man" with a "man's figure" and builds both his house and his family from the ground up. His son Kenyon is less explicitly masculine, partaking in sports only "tokenistically" and is more of a "lanky" boy compared to his father's strong, stoic presence. However, Mr Clutter is not portrayed as a misogynist or oppressively patriarchal force – he cares deeply for his wife as evidenced by his final words, and he even welcomes the thought of his only son pursuing engineering instead of growing up to take over the farm, as was the custom at the time. But where Mr Clutter's brand of masculinity is broadly positive, Perry's conception of it is disastrously destructive.

Prototypical: a perfect example of something, like a prototype.

Perry considers Dick a pinnacle of masculinity, while Perry embodies more stereotypically feminine traits such as being emotionally intelligent, artistic, and prone to crying like the '**weaker sex**.' He is also highly submissive towards Dick, who calls him "honey" and "baby," and is portrayed as being desperate in his search for a male figure of authority he can attach to. This is implied to have stemmed from unresolved issues with his father who, whilst rugged and manly on the surface, was unable to provide much-needed stability in his childhood. This contrasts greatly with the heroic Alvin Dewey, who comforts his children in times of crisis and promises to catch the bad guys so they won't "hurt anybody ever again." Like Clutter, Dewey is not afraid to "bake a cake" or wear an apron despite the traditionally feminine associations these have, indicating they are men who are confident in their own, healthy masculinity.

Weaker sex: a dated term used to characterise women and their perceived 'weaker' attributes.

However, for Dick and Perry, masculinity is a means of asserting power and dominance to mask insecurities, and their struggles to do this effectively only further their mental anguish.

Religion

Our first introduction to religion is that the Clutters are Methodists, while Nancy's boyfriend Bobby is Catholic (which are both denominations of Christianity, but apparently that's not good enough!). Mr Clutter's expectation that Nancy only marry a good Methodist boy like her elder sisters causes some friction in his relationship with her, and we hear from Nancy's diary and her phone call with Susan that Nancy was struggling with these divided loyalties to two people she loves.

Mr Clutter's old hunting buddies are also the first to volunteer for the grisly task of cleaning the murder scenes after the police have finished with them, solemnly heading to the farm with a sense of good "Christian duty." These kinds of references serve to create a sense of the dominant religious paradigm, and hence elevate the crime against the Clutter to a crime against God in the community's mind.

Perry has a far more complex relationship with religion, having sworn off it after being abused by nuns he still thinks of as "Black Widows," but simultaneously pining after people like Don Cullivan and especially Willie-Jay whose religions provide them with a stability Perry craves. However, he is left feeling adrift when he perceives Willie-Jay has abandoned him after leaving prison to live his own life. In his final conversation with Cullivan, he conveys his complete lack of contrition for his actions, which stuns the religious man, and we like Cullivan look on in horror as Perry begs for death, having no faith left.

Section 6

Structural Features Analysis

Genre

Let's start with what should be an easy question: what sort of book is *In Cold Blood?* Most resources and text lists categorise it as 'non-fiction,' but Capote oxymoronically described it as a "non-fiction novel" that "br[ought] to journalism the technique of fiction" – in other words, he wanted to investigate a real story but present it using his storytelling flourish. Though Capote is said to have pioneered this genre of literary journalism, there have been various 'pseudofactual novels' throughout history.

But there are also several things that this book *is not.* For one, it is not a whodunnit, as discussed in the thematic analysis on page 50. It is also not a mystery thriller that overdramatises events and follows a satisfying, familiar narrative structure. Capote jumps from perspective to perspective, even diverting to cite a psychiatric article on trends among mentally ill criminals. Nor is it like a **lurid** slasher film that delights in the gory details of the murders or the executions. Deaths happen swiftly in the novel, and it is their causes and consequences that Capote is concerned with.

In choosing to tell this story at all, Capote is exercising creative intent, as he is composing a work of literature, choosing particular language and deliberately presenting a narrative in a particular way. The genre of *In Cold Blood* is therefore **inextricably** linked with the narrative itself, and with Capote's intentions.

Lurid: shockingly vivid, exaggerated, or sensational.

Inextricable: in a way that cannot be untangled or separated.

Narrative voice

Unlike many other works of non-fiction that blur lines between genres, *In Cold Blood* has very few moments of **authorial intrusion** (a notable exception being when Capote goes on a **diatribe** against the M'Naghten Rule when it is brought up in the trial).

This is not a memoir or autobiographical work about how Capote underwent research and engaged with this story; in fact, you may at first struggle to discuss Capote's views and values in your analysis, as these are much more obtuse than more conventional novels and plays that are chosen as prescribed texts. But as the **omniscient** third person narration weaves stories and voices together, a portrait of the characters and of Holcomb unfolds. This vantage point allows Capote to draw parallels between a vast array of characters, authentically capturing their perspectives and contrasting them with one another.

Authorial intrusion: when an author inserts themselves into the narrative, or interrupts to make their own views apparent.

Diatribe: an angry rant against an idea.

Omniscient: all-knowing.

Quotation marks

Any material in the novel surrounded by quotation marks is taken from official records or transcribed from conversations Capote had. But that is not to say that details outside of these direct quotes are dubious, nor that all quoted information is undoubtedly true. Many of the novel's most reliable sources are paraphrased, and some of the quoted material is fictionalised (or otherwise contested by the real-life individuals involved).

Furthermore, if this book were a research essay, Capote would fail with flying colours! He never clarifies where any of these quotes come from – there are no footnotes or bibliographies! And so with a few exceptions, we are often left to speculate who amongst the living could have provided this information, or how accurate their recollections were.

Foreshadowing

In Cold Blood is written with the advantage of hindsight. Capote (and his contemporary readership who were familiar with the case) are all too aware of the tragic ending, and the fact that "four shotgun blasts... ended six lives." As such, the book is written with a rather **fatalistic** tone, constantly foreshadowing the events that unfolded on the Clutter farm on 15 November, 1959.

Fatalistic: believing that everything is predetermined and inevitable.

The chapter titles are one such way Capote achieves this. Originally the four-part structure of *In Cold Blood* was designed to fit the four-part instalment structure of its original publication in the *New York Times Magazine,* though it would be published a year later in the book format we have today. The first chapter – **The Last to See Them Alive** – is the most ominous, and foreshadows the Clutters' deaths as well as the notion of witnesses to an as yet unknown crime. **Persons Unknown** then chronicles Dick and Perry's time on the run while investigators struggle to piece together the crime; at this point, the fact that the persons are unknown is their greatest concern, though they will soon have to wrestle with the senselessness of their motives in the next chapter, **Answer.** If you look ahead before you start reading, this **pithy** chapter title would seem to foreshadow some kind of resolution where we are given answers to all of our unresolved questions. But then, the looming threat of the final chapter, **The Corner,** awaits. We learn that this is the colloquial name for Kansas' death row, and is hence clearly foreshadowing Dick and Perry's fates.

Pithy: short, succinct, and to the point.

Beyond this, each chapter is littered with ominous references (especially the first chapter!) like Mr Clutter heading for "home and the day's work, unaware that it would be his last," or Mrs Clutter's bible bookmark being embroidered with the quote "Take ye heed, watch and pray: for ye know not when the time is."

Later in the book, such musings take on a more mournful tone, such as Paul Helm's feelings at the Clutter's estate auction being like a "second funeral."

Setting

Much of the first chapter is dedicated to building up our understanding of the town of Holcomb, in many ways unique but in many others universal. The small town is characterised as seeming like an "aimless congregation of buildings" to outsiders who view it as being "out there," but Capote closes this distance by capturing the sense of dilapidation and destitution that has befallen many of its buildings and people. It is also a pitiful but eerie town of contradictions: there is "an electric sign [that says] DANCE – but the dancing had ceased," and an "irrelevant sign [that says] HOLCOMB BANK. The bank failed in 1933." This creates a sense of unease as we are transported to the world of Holcomb which, though undeniably welcoming to all (even the mother of a killer, as we see in their kind treatment towards Mrs Hickock during the trial) is in some small way unnatural as its reputation is so discordant with the violent crime that occurred there.

"Until one morning in mid-November of 1959, few Americans – in fact, few Kansans – had ever heard of Holcomb," but after the events Capote records, he implies few Americans will ever forget it.

Pathetic fallacy

This is a technique used to describe when the external environment mirrors one's internal emotions (e.g. the weather rains when a character is sad). But in fact, what we see in this novel is the opposite of pathetic fallacy – the external world is repeatedly described as being "gloriously bright-skied" after the murder of four innocent people has happened, and that Christmas, there is a "bold sun" and "**azure** sky" as the Clutter's friends are still reeling from the tragedy. This only serves to heighten the horror of what occurs, and emphasises how the extraordinary events seem to contravene the laws of nature.

Azure: bright blue.

Symbolism

Tattoos

Dick and Perry's tattoos represent their personalities: Dick is "self-designed and self-executed" with an assortment of animals, nudes, and mementos, whilst Perry's are professionally done colourful artworks of a tiger, a snake (an animal which he will later describe having haunting dreams about strangling him) and motifs of death like skulls and tombstones. Hence, where Dick almost attempts to mould himself into his lifestyle of criminality, Perry's brand of evil is in some ways more pure and genuine.

Nancy's diary

Nancy's diary is an archetypal teenage girl's journal in which she details the relatively mundane events of her day. It is described by Dewey as containing the "unsensational confidings of an intelligent child who adored animals, who liked to read, cook, sew, dance, ride horseback – a popular, pretty, virginal girl." That she has consistently written in the journal for over four years is a testament to her diligence and self-discipline, as well as her fondness for routines (coupled with her brushing her hair a hundred times each morning and evening). It is also a tragic encapsulation of everything she will never grow up to do or discover, including her future relationship with Bobby or the various extracurricular activities she was preparing for at the time of her death.

We learn that each year she uses a different coloured pen, but also that she consciously and consistently changes her handwriting style, trying to find one that suits her. One of her teachers even remarks that she does this multiple times in her essays – this symbolises Nancy's deliberate quest for a sense of self as she approaches young adulthood.

The yellow bird

This is a hallucination or dream that Perry develops in childhood, likely a form of escapism from his abuse, as he considers it his "hovering avenger" that inflicts his wrath upon those who harm him. He also fantasises about the bird when he contemplates suicide as the bird evolves into a potent symbol of his suffering. Initially, this bird is constructed to be a force for good in Perry's life, though still founded in desires for violence and vengeance. Whether because of this nature or because Perry's mental condition worsens as his journey progresses, the bird is warped into a promise of death as Perry repeatedly engages in suicidal **ideation**. Perry considers the bird a manifestation of Jesus, perhaps representing the religious faith that he never fully grasps due to his trauma with the "Black Widow" nuns (more animal imagery – this time the most venomous spider in America!) whilst some critics view the bird as a symbolic protector, almost like a surrogate parental figure. This is left somewhat ambiguous in the novel.

Ideation: the formation of ideas in one's mind (in this context, contemplating suicide).

Section 7

Quote bank

Justice and the morality of the death penalty

Quote	Chapter
"I believe in capital punishment. It's like the Bible says—an eye for an eye."	3
"It was wrong of me to hate [Perry]; I've got nothing but pity for him now."	3
"I started drinking, and was drunk for almost a month. I neglected my business, spent more money than I earned, wrote bad checks, and in the end became a thief. For this last I was sent to the penitentiary"	4
"It wasn't because of anything the Clutters did. They never hurt me. Like other people. Like people have all my life. Maybe it's just the Clutters were the ones that had to pay for it."	4
"It's a rotten world," Latham said. There's no answer to it but meanness. That's all anybody understands – meanness."	4
"I don't believe in capital punishment, morally or legally."	4

Mental illness and insanity

Quote	Chapter
"There's got to be something wrong with somebody who'd do a thing like that."	2
"She'd fill a tub with ice-cold water, put [Perry] in it, and hold me under till I was blue.'	2

"In some ways, old Perry was "spooky as hell." Take for example, that temper of his. He could slide into a fury "quicker than ten drunk Indians. And yet, you wouldn't know it. "He might be ready to kill you, but you'd never know it, not to look at or listen to."	2
"Look at his family!... His mother, an alcoholic, had strangled on her own vomit... Fern, the other daughter, had jumped out of a window... [and] Jimmy, who had one day driven his wife to suicide and killed himself the next."	2
Floyd "never for a minute believed [Dick] meant to carry it out."	3
"Concussed his head in a car smash-up. After that, he wasn't the same boy. Gambling, writing bad checks, I never knew him to do them things before."	3
"The murderous potential can become activated, especially if some disequilibrium is already present, when the victim-to-be is unconsciously perceived as a key figure in some past traumatic configuration."	4

The American dream

Quote	Chapter
"The village of Holcomb stands on the high wheat plains of Western Kansas, a lonesome area that other Kansans call "out there."	1
"He wore a plain gold band, which was the symbol, a quarter-century old, of his marriage to the person he had wished to marry... Bonnie Fox... She had given him four children – a trio of daughters, then a son."	1
[Herb was] "known for his equanimity, his charitableness, and the fact that he paid good wages."	1
"The handsome white house, standing on an ample lawn of groomed Bermuda grass, impressed Holcomb; it was a place people pointed out."	1

"We went around to the kitchen door, and of course it wasn't locked; the only person who locked doors around there was Mrs. Helm—the family never did."	1
"Nothing can go wrong... Because the plan was Dick's, and from the first footfall to final silence, flawlessly devised."	1
"Look all over the world and you won't find friendlier people or fresher air or sweeter drinking water."	1
"All the neighbors are rattlesnakes... It's the same the whole world over."	2
"After he graduated from high school [Dick] wanted to go on to college. Study to be an engineer. But we couldn't do it. Never had any money."	3
"Strong character, high courage, hard work – it seemed that none of these were a determining factor in the fates of Tex John's children. They shared a doom against which virtue was no defence."	3

Tragedy amidst normality

Quote	Chapter
[The murders] "stimulated fires of mistrust" and "many old neighbours viewed each other strangely, and as strangers."	1
Mr Helm would testify "that... was the last I seen them... nothing out of the ordinary."	1
"The only sure thing is every one of them has got to go."	1
"Strangers, ignorant of the local disaster—were startled by what they saw as they crossed the prairie and passed through Holcomb: windows ablaze, almost every window in almost every house, and, in the brightly lit rooms, fully clothed people, even entire families, who sat the whole night wide awake, watchful, listening."	2
"The head of each [of the Clutter's bodies] was completely encased in cotton... [and] twinkled like Christmas-tree snow."	2

"For the majority of Holcomb's population, having lived for seven weeks amid unwholesome rumours, general mistrust, and suspicion, appeared to feel disappointed at being told that the murderer was not someone among themselves."	3

Senselessness

Quote	Chapter
"Four shotgun blasts that, all told, ended six human lives."	1
"The Clutters were the least likely to be murdered."	1
"I'd been too dazed, too numb, to feel the full viciousness of it. The suffering. The horror. They were dead. A whole family. Gentle, kindly people, people *I* knew – *murdered.* You had to believe it, because it was really true."	1
"I frisked the girl's room, and I found a little purse, like a doll's purse. Inside it was a silver dollar. I dropped it somehow, and it rolled across the floor. Rolled under a chair. I had to get down on my knees. And then it was like I was outside myself. Watching myself in some nutty movie. It made me sick. [. . .] here I am crawling on my belly to steal a child's silver dollar. One dollar. And I'm crawling on my belly to get it."	3
"I knelt down beside Mr. Clutter and the pain of kneeling—I thought of that goddam dollar. Silver dollar. The shame. Disgust... But I didn't realise what I'd done until I heard the sound. Like somebody drowning"	3
The Clutter robbery amounted to "between forty and fifty dollars."	4

Masculinity

Quote	Chapter
Herb "cut a man's man figure" and was "always certain of what he wanted from the world."	1
"Mr. Clutter had of necessity learned to cook... and was excellent at it – no woman in Kansas baked a better loaf of salt-rising bread, and his celebrated coconut cookies were the first to go at charity cake sales"	1
"Dick's literalness, his pragmatic approach to every subject... made Dick seem, compared to [Perry], so authentically tough, invulnerable, 'totally masculine'."	1
"Just nothing scares you," she said, commenting on a generally recognized quality of Mr. Clutter's: a fearless self-assurance that set him apart, and while it created respect, also limited the affections of others a little. "I can't imagine you afraid. No matter what happened, you'd talk your way out of it."	1
"That Dick had married – married twice – and fathered three sons was something he envied. A wife, children – those were experiences a man ought to have."	2
"When Alvin was sheriff, I know some of the boys teased him, Used to say, 'Lookayonder! Here comes Sheriff Dewey! Tough guy! Totes a six-shooter! But once he gets home, off comes the gun and on goes the apron!'"	2
"All the same, [Barbara's father] was 'a real man'."	3
"Of course, Dick was a blowhard; his toughness existed solely in situations where he unarguably had the upper hand."	3

Religion

Quote	Chapter
"He did not smoke, and of course he did not drink; indeed, he had never tasted spirits, and was inclined to avoid people who had... [Herb's social circle] was supplied by the members of Garden City's First Methodist Church, [. . .] most of whom were as abstemious as Mr. Clutter could desire."	1
"Though [Bonnie Clutter] subscribed to several periodicals, [. . .] none of these rested on her bedside table—only a Bible."	1
"Take ye heed, watch and pray: for ye know not when the time is."	1
"Perry decided to speak out; he was sorry, but it was not for him—heaven, hell, saints, divine mercy—and if Willie-Jay's affection was founded on the prospect of Perry's someday joining him at the foot of the Cross, then he was deceived and their friendship false."	1
"But that's impossible. Can you imagine Mr. Clutter missing church? Just to sleep?"	1
"For, feeling it their duty, a Christian task, these men had volunteered to clean [the Clutter house]"	2
"Let us forgive as God would have us do. It is not right that we hold a grudge in our hearts. The doer of the act is going to find it difficult indeed to live with himself. His only peace of mind will be when he goes to God for forgiveness."	2
"I never considered death or the possibility of a life hereafter. And this is why I'm writing to you: because God made you as well as me and He loves you just as He loves me."	4
"That stuff don't ring true with me. I can't accept overnight what I've always denied. The truth is, you've done more for me than anyway what you call God ever has. Or ever will. By writing to me, by signing yourself 'friend'."	4
"May the Lord have mercy on your soul."	4

Section 8

Sample Essays

Essay One

QUESTION: *In Cold Blood* is about tragedy. Discuss.

ESSAY	COMMENTS
INTRODUCTION Silhouetted against a backdrop of a 1950s rural community ruled by hopes of the American Dream, *In Cold Blood* is the distillation of an American nightmare – a senseless and unpredictable tragedy in the form of the brutal killing of four innocent citizens. By foregrounding the aftermath of this tragedy, Capote's nonfiction novel is a complex examination of *mens rea*[1] and the nuances of having a punishment fit a crime. Hence, *In Cold Blood* is not just about *one* tragedy and the death of the innocent Clutters, but also the very *notion* of tragedy[2] as a source of conflict, fear, and apprehension.	1. This is a Latin term you may recognise if you do Legal Studies! It means 'guilty mind' and refers to the intentionality of a crime, which must be proven in criminal cases. 2. This prompt is one some students will despise for being so open ended, but in many ways this is a great opportunity to explore the substantial theme of 'tragedy' with almost complete freedom. Here, I'm choosing to look at how the text goes beyond the tragedy of these four deaths and forces us to confront even greater tragedies like mortality and meaninglessness.

PARAGRAPH 1 From the text's very beginning, Capote conveys an imminent sense of a lasting tragedy. The first chapter title, "The Last to see Them Alive"[3] ominously heralds the impending deaths of as yet unknown individuals, whilst also planting in readers' minds the thought of witnesses to what will be made clear was an horrific crime. Much of this chapter is then dedicated to depicting the quotidian lives of the likeable Clutters. In particular, Capote builds up our perception of Mr Clutter as the archetypal American patriarch, just as Mr Clutter builds his own "handsome white house" from the ground up – a very literal demonstration of the American dream[4] and how any individual can make something of themselves. By contrast, the story Capote tells of Perry Smith[5] reveals him as an individual who lacked these strong foundations, or any sort of childhood stability. The loving Clutter home is a far cry from the abuse and hardships Perry endures at the hands of "Black Widow" nuns – sinister symbols of venomous creates that come close to killing him by drowning him in " ice-cold water." Subsequently, he is afflicted with a "shared... doom" and family curse of mental illness, against which "virtue was no defence." This highlights the flaws in the notion of the American Dream as being within reach of any individual, regardless of their circumstances. Tragically, Perry's actions lead to the loss of a loving family from their community, but Capote also suggests the pain of this absence exists in Perry too as a fractured "wounded creature" who lacked a loving family of his own.	3. Chapter titles can make for excellent supplementary evidence in your body paragraphs, especially when considering the atmosphere Capote creates, or the consistent foreshadowing of tragedy throughout the novel. 4. This contextual reference strengthens the argument without getting too distracted by this external idea. Remember, you don't need to go into great detail defining things like the American Dream – just make sure you use it confidently in your essays and then shift your focus to textual evidence. 5. Try to avoid only having one character in a body paragraph; though at times this can allow you to do a 'deep dive' into one particular individual, more often you'll be able to construct a better argument if you give yourself the chance to compare and contrast, as we have done here with Mr Clutter and Perry.

PARAGRAPH 2

In Cold Blood also explicates the confronting nature of a tragedy happening without warning and amidst such mundane circumstances. Nancy Clutter's diary,[6] containing the "unsensational confidings" of a teenager, are not only a distillation of unfulfilled potential and possibility, but an otherwise normal life now frozen in time. She and her father will never resolve their minor conflict over Bobby's Catholicism being at odds with their Methodist faith, and Nancy will never realise her dreams of pursuing tertiary studies, nor will she even have the opportunity to be "grown-up enough to be one person with one kind of signature." Her otherwise ordinary musings about how she wishes it will be "summer here.... forever" take on a tragic dramatic irony as her life is cut short. Later, when Larry Hendricks gives his account of discovering the bodies, he remarks that Kenyon "haunts [him] the most" since he "was the most recognisable" in his T-shirt and blue jeans, unremarkable clothing[7] that belies his inordinately violent death, shot in the face with a shotgun. In the aftermath of the family's "mass burial," the town shifts to a new normal, wracked with suspicion, survivor's guilt, and a fear of their own mortality. Even when Dick and Perry are caught, there are some, like Myrtle Clare, who cannot relinquish their suspicions that there was some grander conspiracy involving people from town, as they have adjusted to a paradigm of mistrust in one another. Hence, Capote explicates the many personal tragedies that unfold over the course of the novel.

6. Combining your analysis of quotes with references to symbols is a great way to showcase the breadth of your textual knowledge and analytical abilities. Also, remember that you can use a piece of evidence to explore more than one idea. Here, we spend a few sentences teasing out the implications of Nancy's diary and the kinds of tragedies this encapsulates, so don't feel like you have to move on too quickly if there's more you can explore that is still relevant to the prompt.

7. This might seem like a very obvious point, but you have to adequately explain yourself in order to get credit for your ideas. The assessor can't fill in the gaps for you, so make sure you guide them along your train of thought by explaining the significance of evidence like this.

PARAGRAPH 3	
Indeed some of the most evocative moments of tragedy in the novel come in unexpected moments, and in startlingly personal ways.[8] One of the scenes in which Perry is most struck by a sense of foolish futility when he "crawl[s] on [his] belly" to "steal a child's silver dollar" when he and Dick fail to find any substantial sums in the Clutter household. This moment of reflection mirrors his confession to Agent Duntz that the pair only made out with "forty or fifty dollars," which Capote portrays as woefully insufficient to justify the deaths of four people. Furthermore, he expounds on the unduly tragic death of Mrs Clutter.[9] She is a woman tormented by chronic postnatal depression, fearing that her children "don't need [her]" with her worst fear being that they and her husband will one day remember her as a "kind of ghost," though tragically, she and her family meet an even worse fate. Though Capote does not dwell on this fact, Mrs Clutter is the last to die, and would have heard all three of the gunshots that killed her beloved husband and children. Perry crudely remarks that she may have "welcomed their swift approach" after all she had heard, though Marie Dewey's dream about Mrs Clutter's restless spirit murmuring "To be murdered. No. No. There's nothing worse. Nothing worse than that. Nothing" implies that her lengthy mental and physical suffering did not make death a relief.[10] The tragedy of Bonnie Clutter is that she suffered in both life and death, with no solace for the survivors to find in either of these realities.	8. This topic sentence signals that we are building off of the previous discussion and arriving at our ultimate argument as we approach the end of the essay. 9. It is quite easy to talk about the Clutters as a tragic collective, but there are lots of analytical opportunities if you discuss them as individuals too. Capote deliberately provides us with these evocative, but limited insights into their lives before they are killed, so you can use these as highly significant evidence of their personalities, experiences, and individual tragedies. 10. This brings together a range of different evidence from multiple sources across the text to strengthen our overarching contention.

CONCLUSION Capote's *In Cold Blood* contains a range of tragedies, varying in scope and severity, though they are all inextricably connected to one another. This underlying tragedy[11] – that suffering begets suffering and that violence and abuse can be unbreakably cyclical – forms part of Capote's poignant narrative, designed to show readers[12] the inevitable entanglements of tragic events that resound across lives and stories alike.	11. Finally, we end by asserting our thesis statement, making sure to focus on the text as a whole, and what Capote achieves or communicates. 12. It is also particularly impressive if you can say something about the overall effect the text has on readers, especially if this is something you can tie in with the core focus of the prompt.

Essay Two

QUESTION: To what extent is Capote's account of the crime accurate and reliable?

ESSAY	COMMENTS
INTRODUCTION *In Cold Blood* is a seminal work of true crime fiction with Capote proudly declaring "every word" to be faithful to the real-life story of the Clutters and their killers. However, the text has also been criticised for potential omissions, fabrications, and biases that altered the narrative in order to suit Capote's agenda.[1] Whilst his research created an undeniably realistic account of the events that took place in Kansas during those fateful years, the novel is also a construct formed by Capote's own views and experiences, and hence its reliability is somewhat ambiguous.[2]	1. This establishes a carefully considered starting point – we are not completely agreeing or disagreeing with the core of the prompt, nor are we fence-sitting. 2. Note that we're not completely giving away our whole contention here, as the final judgement will come in our conclusion. This can be a great way to give your essay a sense of progress (i.e. acknowledge that something is complex, nuanced, or ambiguous in your introduction, and then provide your specific thesis about what this means at the end of your essay). Just make sure you don't run out of time in exam conditions!

PARAGRAPH 1

On the surface, the fact that Capote shifts between multiple perspectives[3] over the course of the text would seem to add credence to the accuracy of his account. However, these deliberate authorial choices are still used to convey certain impressions to the readers. Most notably, Capote chooses[4] to have us follow English teacher Larry Hendricks as he uncovers the horrors of the Clutter family murder scenes. Hendricks is our guide, but we are also told he "wanted to write" stories like his idol Ernest Hemingway. This could be interpreted as a warning sign about his penchant for constructed narratives, but instead, Capote includes Hendricks' recollection that he consciously told himself to "make a note of every detail... in case [he] was ever called on to testify in court." What follows is an incredibly precise, methodical, and harrowing description of the men who find the bodies. In this sense, although the ideology and views on justice and punishment later in the text may be more based on Capote's point of view, he takes care to establish the veracity of the facts of the case as the novel's foundation.[5]

3. Remember that you are not just limited to talking about plot points, characters, and quotes as your evidence. Any structural feature or textual element you can find to analyse is valid, and in fact, combining a discussion of things like the text's omniscient narration or symbolism *with* more conventional evidence like quotes will be all the more impressive to your marker!

4. Try to frame things like this in the context of Capote's authorial intent. It's not that 'Larry discovers the bodies' – it's that 'Capote chooses to have us follow the character of Larry as he discovers the bodies.' This subtle distinction goes a long way in showcasing your understanding of the text as a construct.

5. This is a solid first body paragraph, as it establishes an opening that is supported by evidence, but hints at subsequent sub-arguments that require further exploration.

PARAGRAPH 2	
Comparatively, Capote departs from the perspectives of the people of Holcomb towards the end of the text, where he more freely opines on the flaws of the justice system.[6] When Dr Jones is called to testify that Dick was able to distinguish right from wrong at the time of the crimes, he is "confined... by the M'Naughten Rule" which, Capote interjects is "a formula quite colourblind to any permutations between black and white." He is legally unable to elaborate, so is dismissed, though Capote posits what Dr Jones "would have testified... had he been allowed to speak further," detailing a complex medical history of brain damage and unusual patterns of behaviour. Here, Capote implies, the law does these men a disservice by not allowing the wider story to be made apparent. This is one of the text's few blatant moments of authorial intrusion,[7] and though it is drawn from accurate medical records, it renders Capote a less reliably unbiased narrator, as readers are exposed to his critique of society's views towards mental illness in the justice system.	6. This topic sentence clearly introduces the next focal point, but it also establishes a connection between this sub-argument and the previous one, giving the essay a clear sense of progression. 7. This is a good use of metalanguage to describe a structural and genre feature of the text, while still maintaining a fluent analytical flow.

PARAGRAPH 3

Ultimately then,[8] Capote's presentation of the Clutter's story is broadly accurate, but not above questioning. Some parts of the novel are surrounded by quotation marks – we only sometimes know who the sources of these quotes are, and even then we can rarely be sure whether these are taken from "official records" or, as Capote says in his Acknowledgements, his "own observation [and] interviews." As he famously boasted about not needing to take notes during such proceedings, readers are unable to completely trust in the legitimacy of these insights. Fittingly, for a story about mankind's desperate search for meaning, the veracity of the book is something readers may never be fully sure about, as there are conflicting reports by Capote, the individuals he interviewed, and people who subsequently interviewed these people after the book's publication. To this end,[9] *In Cold Blood* is a text fraught with questions of accuracy and reliability, both within its subject matter and in it's overarching structure as a construct of Capote's.

8. I really like using this phrase in my last body paragraph; although I'm not technically concluding the essay just yet, this implies a sense of finality in this argument as we tie the threads of our contention and sub-ideas together.

9. By the end of your third or final body paragraph, you should be prepared to make a statement like this that sets the foundation for your conclusion.

CONCLUSION

Though the novel is incontestably fixated on accuracy, and largely driven by a desire to provide a faithful account of the murders and their aftermath, Capote's text is not infallible, as readers are made to appreciate the value of perspective and the untenable possibility of a completely accurate rendition of such a complex story.[10]

10. As always, your conclusion can be relatively straightforward – just round off the discussion by ending with some insight into the intention or interpretation of the text, and make sure to use Capote's name to highlight this focus.

Essay Three

QUESTION: How does Capote convey the horror of what happened to the Clutters?

ESSAY	COMMENTS
INTRODUCTION *In Cold Blood,* true to its subtitle, is a story of "a multiple murder and its consequences,"[1] and it is by capturing these ramifications that Capote conveys the horror of the Clutter case. Through the omniscient narration[2] of his non-fiction novel, Capote weaves together perspectives and voices to create a tapestry of tragedy, and to reveal to readers the senselessness of both a desire for violence and a desire for retribution.	1. Remember that you can use 'paratextual' information (i.e. things from elsewhere in the text, such as the Acknowledgements) to supplement your analysis of the primary material. 2. This is hinting at the kinds of structural features we will use as evidence to answer the 'how' part of this question.

PARAGRAPH 1	
The fatalistic tone[3] of *In Cold Blood* amplifies the sense of tragedy in the events it depicts. As much of Capote's contemporary readership[4] would have been intimately familiar with the case in which "four shotgun blasts... ended six lives,"[5] he constantly foreshadows the tragic end of the Clutters and their killers alike. In our introduction to Mr Clutter, we are told he heads "home and the day's work, unaware that it would be his last," which forewarns readers of the imminent tragedy. Uniquely, Capote also shifts perspectives throughout this chapter to reveal to us the perpetrators of this tragedy, though they too are ill-prepared for what is about to unfold. Perry's faith in Dick's plan that is apparently "from first footfall to final silence, flawlessly devised" is quickly undermined in his mind and ours when the two men are unable to anticipate how much rope they will need to tie up an unknown number of potential guests at the Clutter household. That some of their bodies are later found tied up with the cord of a Venetian blind is evidence of frantic improvisation, and Larry Henricks' account of the morbid discoveries in each room draw our attention to how many things are out of place or otherwise inexplicable. Through this, Capote therefore establishes an atmosphere of bewildered perplexity at both the nature and motives behind the murders that will persist throughout the novel.	3. Try to add lots of metalanguage throughout your body paragraphs, as this consistently showcases your analytical understanding of the text. 4. It is also valuable to refer to the reception of the text amongst readers and critics (in moderation). The majority of your essay should focus on the novel itself, but you can integrate your background knowledge when relevant to add more sophistication to the discussion. 5. Make sure you modify quotes and omit any information that does not directly help you make your argument. This ensures you have an easier time memorising textual information (as you only have to remember the important stuff!) but it also proves to your examiner that you can be precise in your use of language and evidence.

PARAGRAPH 2	
Furthermore, the consequences of the Clutters' deaths reverberate through the town of Holcomb in tragically poignant ways. Having portrayed the Clutters – particularly Herb and Nancy – as being central pillars in their community, Capote magnifies the void they leave behind. These social and emotional consequences are especially evident in Nancy's friends Susan and Nancy Ewalt,[6] as well as her boyfriend Bobby. That the two girls are the ones to find their friend's body is already an incredibly confronting detail in the text, and Capote's description of their recollections during the trial involving a bitterly ironic juxtaposition of "sunshine in a bedroom, and their schoolmate, Nancy Clutter, surrounded by her own blood" suggests they are both dealing with lasting trauma. The novel also provides various vignettes from the people of Holcomb who have to come to terms with not just the loss of their friends and neighbours, but the ensuing suspicion and mistrust in the wake of this. Through the depth and breadth of these perspectives, Capote implies[7] the effects of the Clutter's deaths were widespread, and long lasting, affecting the collecting psyche of Holcomb as a microcosm for America as a whole.	6. These are two relatively minor characters, but are still vitally important in this particular discussion. Though the assessors never have an expectation that you will bring up specific pieces of evidence, you would be wise to memorise a wide range so that you can draw from whatever seems most relevant. The long list of characters in this novel works to your advantage here, as you can streamline your study by focusing on finding something to analyse about each of the minor characters, as well as more substantial lists of ideas from major ones. 7. Concluding your paragraphs with a statement of authorial intent (i.e. using Capote's name and a verb like 'implies,' 'highlights,' 'emphasises,' etc.) is a strong way to bring your argument back to the prompt and your contention.

PARAGRAPH 3

This culminates[8] in the text's final horror: the executions of Dick and Perry, and the relative lack of solace this provides the survivors. Curiously, the remaining Clutter children, Eveanna and Beverly, do not attend either the trial or the hanging. Whilst this could be interpreted as the result of not wanting to confront such traumas anew, perhaps Capote is instead endorsing their decisions to move on with their lives. In this sense, Beverly's decision to get married just days after the murders while the family is still in town is not morbid, but an admirable commitment to overcome horror and restore some sense of normality and continuity to life. By contrast, Dewey and the KBI team do attend the hanging, but are left with a hollow feeling as they watch Perry, "an exiled animal, a creature walking wounded," later haunted by the dead man's "small booted... childish feet, tilted, dangling." Through this, Capote forces us to confront the psychological horror that what was done to the Clutters cannot be undone with the deaths of Dick and Perry. Rather, the horror at the heart of the novel is that this senseless tragedy befell and innocent family, and that some things could never be made right, and we must, like Dewey, "leav[e] behind [us] the big sky and the overwhelming reality of mortality.

8. As always, we prepare to end the discussion by ensuring our last body paragraph feels like a summation of the argument, adding more evidence but also tying things together so that we can reach an overwhelmingly strong conclusion.

CONCLUSION

Ultimately, Capote's *In Cold Blood* explores various different ramifications of the Clutter murders, forcing readers to face not only the horror of what humanity is capable of inflicting, but also the manifold unintended and unexpected consequences this has on society.[9]

The conclusion itself can be pretty sort, especially if your final body paragraph has already done some of the work in 'zooming out' to authorial intent and the bigger picture of the text, but it must be powerful!